Light of the World

Benedict XVI

Light of the World

The Pope, the Church, and the Signs of the Times

A Conversation with Peter Seewald

Translated by
Michael J. Miller and Adrian J. Walker

CATHOLIC TRUTH SOCIETY
LONDON

IGNATIUS PRESS   SAN FRANCISCO

Original German edition:
Licht der Welt: Der Papst, die Kirche und die Zeichen der Zeit:
Ein Gespräch mit Peter Seewald
© 2010 by Libreria Editrice Vaticana, Vatican City

Preface, chapters 1–7, and the appendix on Benedict XVI's
curriculum vitae and chronology translated by Michael J. Miller.
Chapters 8–18 translated by Adrian J. Walker.

Cover: Photograph of Pope Benedict XVI: © Stefano Spaziani

Front cover design by Roxanne Mei Lum
Back cover design by John Herreid

© Libreria Editrice Vaticana

Published in USA © 2010 by Ignatius Press, San Francisco

Published in the UK and Republic of Ireland 2010
by the Incorporated Catholic Truth Society, London
ISBN 978-1-86082-709-9
www.cts-online.org.uk

*God looks down from heaven upon the sons of men,
to see if there are any that are wise, that seek after God....
They eat God's bread,
But they do not call upon his name.*
Psalm 53:3–5

Contents

Appendix

Foreword

George Weigel

The Chair of Peter affords its occupant a unique view of the human condition, unlike that offered to any other global figure from any other vantage point.

World political leaders see the flow of history in terms of interests, alliances, and power. Intellectuals of international repute perceive humanity in terms of their philosophical, historical, or scientific theories. Leaders of great commercial enterprises analyze the world in terms of markets to be penetrated. World-renowned entertainers imagine their audiences in terms of the emotions they seek to evoke.

Popes, if they have the wit and the stomach for it, see the whole picture—the entirety of the human drama, in both its nobility and its wickedness. And they see it through the prism of humanity's origins and humanity's ultimate destiny.

It can be a dizzying, even disorienting, view. Over almost two millennia of papal history, some Popes have indeed bent history to their wills—or, perhaps more accurately, to the power of their faith; one thinks immediately of John Paul II's pivotal role in the collapse of European Communism. Other Popes have seemed overwhelmed by the tides of history, their papacies swamped by riptides they were unable to channel or resist. Novelist Morris West once wrote that the Chair of Peter "...was a high leap, halfway out of the world and into a vestibule of divinity. The man who wore the Fisherman's ring and the triple tiara carried also the sins of the world like a leaden cope on his shoulders. He stood on a lonely pinnacle, alone, with the spread carpet of the nations before him, and above, the naked face of the Almighty. Only a fool would envy him the power and the glory and the terror of such a principality." West exaggerated, as novelists tend to do, but he caught something of the unique perspective on humanity and its pilgrimage through history that the papacy thrusts before a man.

Having worked closely with John Paul II for almost a quarter-century, and having written incisively about the Office of Peter for decades before that, Joseph Ratzinger knew all this when the question was put to him on April 19, 2005, two days after his seventy-eighth birthday: *"Acceptasne electionem de te canonice factam in Summum Pontificem?"* [Do you accept your canonical election as Supreme Pontiff?] The world and the Church can be grateful that, once again, Ratzinger put his own plans on hold—this time, permanently—by saying Yes to that awesome query. For Joseph Ratzinger, Pope Benedict XVI, brings both a clear-eyed view and the courage of convictions born in faith and honed by reason to the papacy's unique vantage point on the human race in the first decades of the twenty-first century.

What the Pope sees, and what he discusses with frankness, clarity, and compassion in this stimulating conversation with Peter Seewald, is a world that (to borrow from Lutheran theologian Robert Jenson) has lost its story: a world in which the progress promised by the humanisms of the past three centuries is now gravely threatened by understandings of the human person that reduce our humanity to a congeries of cosmic chemical accidents: a humanity with no intentional origin, no noble destiny, and thus no path to take through history. This is not, it must be emphasized, the cranky view of a man ill at ease in the postmodern world. Rather, as Benedict XVI takes pains to underscore in this conversation, his challenge to postmodernity is one intended to preserve and extend the achievements of modernity, not least in the sphere of political freedom—and to do so by encouraging postmodernity to rediscover some ancient truths about itself.

Those truths include the necessary dialogue between faith and reason. Faith devoid of reason risks becoming superstition and blind prejudice. Reason inattentive to faith risks solipsism, self-absorption, detachment from reality. The effects of faith detached from reason are all around us: thus Benedict's urgent challenge to Islam. So are the effects of reason inattentive to faith: thus Benedict's challenge, to a West in cultural disarray, to rediscover the biblical roots of the Western civilizational project. Like John Paul II, Benedict XVI sees both facets of this dual crisis of world civilization clearly; and, again like the predecessor to whom he pays touching tribute in this book, he has put these issues on the table of the world's conversation as no one else has or can.

Benedict XVI brought to the papacy more than a half-century of reflection on the truths of biblical faith and a master teacher's capacity to explicate those truths and bring them to bear on contemporary situations in a luminously clear way. I have had the privilege of knowing many men and women of high intelligence, even genius, in my lifetime; I have never known anyone like Benedict XVI, who, when one asks him a question, pauses, thinks carefully, and then answers in complete paragraphs—often in his third, fourth, or fifth language. Peter Seewald's well-crafted questions give Benedict XVI good material with which to work. But it is the remarkably lucid and precise mind of Joseph Ratzinger that makes the papal answers here sing.

Those who had known Joseph Ratzinger in his pre-papal days knew this about him, as they had known him for a man of exquisite manners and a pastor's kind heart. Which is to say, those who knew the man knew that the caricature of him in the world press—a caricature created by his ecclesiastical enemies in a particularly nasty exercise of *odium theologicum*—was just that: a caricature, a cartoon, with no tether to the real man. Happily, the world has been able to discover this since April 19, 2005.

Those with eyes to see and ears to hear have discovered a pastor who meets, prays, and weeps with those suffering the aftereffects of being abused by men they thought were their shepherds; and by the victims' own testimony, the tears were real, as was the Pope's horror and anguish at what his brothers in the priesthood had done and what his brothers in the episcopate had failed to address. Those willing to hear and see have met a world-class intellectual who, in addressing British Catholic school-children, distills sixty years of higher learning into a winsome and compelling catechetical message on how important it is to become a twenty-first-century saint. Those who come to Rome to attend one of Benedict XVI's general audiences have encountered a master catechist, whose command of the Bible, the Fathers, and the theological traditions of Christian West and Christian East is simply unparalleled—as is his capacity to explicate what he has learned in ways that virtually everyone can understand and engage.

That is the Benedict XVI whom the reader will meet in *Light of the World*: a teacher to whom any sensible person would want to give a fair hearing. That this teacher is also a pastor, and a thoroughgoing Christian disciple who believes that friendship with Jesus is the key to human happiness, suggests that, like his predecessor, Benedict XVI is reforming the papacy by returning it to its evangelical roots as an office of witness to the truth of God in Christ.

Benedict XVI lived through the trauma of the mid-twentieth century, in which false conceptions of the human person and human destiny almost destroyed civilization, as he lived through the drama of the late twentieth century, which saw the end of Communism and a brief moment of optimism about the human future. He sees a world that, contrary to that optimism, has tended to shutter its windows and lock its doors against the light: the light of truth, the light of Christ, the light of God in whom there is no darkness. To vary the imagery, Benedict, from the unique vantage point of the papacy, sees a world yearning for love but attaching itself to false loves. To this, he counterposes that with which Dante closed the greatest poem ever written: *"l'amor che move il sole e l'altre stelle"* [the Love that moves the sun and the other stars].

Benedict XVI has met this Love, embraced it, and given his life to sharing it. It is loving this Love that has made Joseph Ratzinger—again, contrary to the cartoon—a joyful man, who wants others to share in the joy of the Lord. He knows full well, as he puts it to Peter Seewald, that we all live "the Christian situation, this battle between two kinds of love." At the moment, it seems to him that, in many parts of the world he surveys, the false loves have gained the upper hand. But he also knows that "love is the key to Christianity" and that true loves, and Love itself, will win the final triumph, which has already been revealed in the Resurrection. Our task, he reminds us, is not to demand immediate victories, but to bear witness to the truth, the love, and the joy that comes from conversion to Christ.

For such a reminder, and for such a witness, Christians, and indeed all men and women of good will, can only be grateful.

George Weigel
Distinguished Senior Fellow
William E. Simon Chair in Catholic Studies
Ethics and Public Policy Center, Washington, D.C.

Preface

Castel Gandolfo in the summer. The way to the Pope's residence led over lonely country roads. In the fields the grain swayed in a gentle breeze, and in the hotel where I had reserved a room a happy wedding party was dancing. Only the lake below in the hollow seemed peaceful and calm, as big and blue as the sea.

As Prefect of the Congregation for the Doctrine of the Faith, Joseph Ratzinger had twice granted me the opportunity to interview him over the course of several days. The Church must not hide, was his attitude; the faith must be explained; and it can be explained, because it is reasonable. He impressed me as being young and modern, not a bean-counter, but rather a man who ventures bravely and retains his curiosity. A masterful teacher, and a disconcerting one as well, because he sees that we are losing things that we really cannot do without.

In Castel Gandolfo some things were different. A cardinal is a cardinal, and the Pope is the Pope. Never before in the history of the Church had a Pontiff answered questions in the form of a personal, direct interview. The mere fact of this conversation sets an important new tone. Benedict XVI had agreed to be at my disposal during his vacation, from Monday through Saturday of the last week in July, for one hour each day. Yet, I reflected, how candid would his answers turn out to be? How does he judge his work thus far? What else does he have planned?

Dark clouds had gathered over the Catholic Church. The scandal of sexual abuse cast its shadow on Benedict's pontificate as well. I was interested in the causes of these things, in the handling of them, but at the same time also in the pressing concerns of the Pope in a decade that scientists believe is going to be absolutely decisive for the overall future of the planet.

The crisis of the Church is one thing, the crisis of society another. The two are not unconnected. Some have reproached Christians, since their religion is an illusory world. But are we not acquainted today with very different worlds that are in fact illusory? The illusory worlds of financial markets, the media, luxury items and fashions? Are we not being forced to witness, painfully, a modern world that is losing its standards and values and is in danger of sinking into the abyss? That is evident in a banking system that is destroying the colossal wealth of the people. There is life in the fast lane, which is literally making us sick. There is the universe of the Internet, for which we do not yet have any answers. Where are we actually going? Are we really allowed to do everything we are able to do?

And when we look into the future: How will the next generation cope with the problems that we are leaving to it? Have we sufficiently prepared and trained them? Does it have a foundation that provides the security and strength to weather even stormy times?

The question is also this: If Christianity in the West is losing its power to shape society, who or what is replacing it? A non-religious "civil society" that no longer tolerates any reference to God in its constitution? A radical atheism that vehemently fights against the values of Judeo-Christian culture?

In every era there has been an attempt to declare God dead, to turn to things that were supposedly more comprehensible, even if they were golden calves. The Bible is full of stories like that. They have less to do with the insufficient attractiveness of faith than with the forces of temptation. But where, then, is a society distanced from God, a godless society headed? Did the twentieth century not just carry out that experiment in the West and the East? With its terrible consequences for the peoples that were afflicted: the smokestacks in the concentration camps, the murderous gulags?

The director of the papal residence, a very friendly elderly man, led me through seemingly endless rooms. He had been acquainted with John XXIII and all his successors, he whispered to me; this one here, he said, is an unusually fine Pope—and inconceivably hard-working.

We waited in an antechamber big as a riding hall. A short time later a door opened. And there stood the not exactly gigantic figure of the Pope, who held out his hand to me. His forces had diminished, he said by way of a greeting, almost apologetically. But then there was no sign at all that the strain of office had really affected the vigor of this man, much less his charisma. Quite the contrary.

As a cardinal, Joseph Ratzinger used to warn about the loss of identity, of orientation, of truth that would result if a new paganism were to take control of people's thoughts and actions. He criticized the narrow-mindedness of a "society of greed" that dares less and less to hope and no longer to believe. It was important, he said, to develop a new sensitivity toward a threatened creation, to oppose the forces of destruction decisively.

Nothing has changed along these lines. Today, as Pope, he wants his Church to submit to a kind of thorough housecleaning after the terrible cases of abuse and other aberrations. What is indispensable, after so many fruitless discussions and a debilitating concern with herself, is finally to become reacquainted with the mystery of the Gospel, Jesus Christ, in all his cosmic greatness. In this crisis of the Church there is a tremendous opportunity, namely, to rediscover what is authentically Catholic. The task is to show God to the people and to tell them the truth. The truth about the mysteries of creation. The truth about human existence. And the truth about our hope, which goes beyond merely worldly matters.

Have we not long since trembled at what we have wrought? The ecological catastrophe continues unchecked. The decline of culture assumes menacing forms. With the medical and technological manipulation of human life, which was once considered sacred, the final boundaries are violated.

At the same time we long for a world that is reliable and trustworthy, that is close and human and protects us in little things and makes the big things accessible to us. Does not the current situation, which often seems so apocalyptic, all but force us to reflect once more about some fundamental things? Where we come from. Where we are going. To ask those questions that are seemingly banal—and that nevertheless burn so inextinguishably in the heart that no generation can get around them? Questions about the meaning of life. About the end of the world. About the Second Coming of Christ, as it is proclaimed in the Gospel.

Six hours interviewing the Pope is a lot of time, and yet six hours is also very little. Within the framework of this discussion only a few questions could be addressed and many could not be answered in depth. In authorizing the text, the Pope did not change the spoken word and made only small corrections where he considered greater factual precision necessary.

The message of Benedict XVI, however, is in the end a dramatic appeal to the Church and the world, to each individual: There is no way we can possibly continue as before, he exclaims. Mankind stands at a crossroads. It is time for reflection. Time for change. Time for conversion. And unwaveringly he maintains: "There are so many problems that all have to be solved but that will not all be solved unless God stands in the center and becomes visible again in the world."

The answer given to this question, "whether God exists—the God of Jesus Christ—and is acknowledged, or whether he disappears", is deciding today, "in this dramatic situation, the fate of the world".

For today's life-style, positions of the sort that are advocated by the Catholic Church have become a monstrous provocation. We have grown accustomed to regarding traditional, time-tested viewpoints and behavior as something that ought to be done away with in favor of cheap trends. The Pope believes, however, that the age of relativism—a world view "that does not recognize anything as definitive and whose ultimate standard consists solely of one's own ego and desires"—is gradually coming to an end. Today, at any rate, a growing number of people cherish the Church not only for her liturgy but also for her resistance; and meanwhile, after a lot of "just going through the motions", a transformation of awareness is becoming evident: people are beginning again to take Christian witness seriously and also to live their religion authentically.

As for the Pope himself: "What is it like", I was asked, "suddenly to sit very close, right across from him?" It reminded me of Émile Zola, who in one of his novels describes a priest who waits, trembling and almost paralyzed, for an audience with Leo XIII. Now with Benedict XVI there is no need to tremble. He makes it remarkably easy for the visitor. This is no Prince of the Church, but rather a servant of the Church, a great giver who completely exhausts himself in his giving.

Sometimes he looks a bit skeptically at you. Over his eyeglasses. Seriously, attentively. And if you are listening to him and sitting beside him, then you not only sense the precision of his thinking and the hope that comes from faith, but then also in a special way a radiance from the light of the world becomes visible, from the face of Jesus Christ, who wants to encounter each one of us and excludes no one.

Munich, October 15, 2010   *Peter Seewald*

PART I

SIGNS OF THE TIMES

1. Popes Do Not Fall from the Sky

Holy Father, on April 16, 2005, your seventy-eighth birthday, you told your co-workers how much you were looking forward to your retirement. Three days later you were the leader of the universal Church with 1.2 billion members. Not exactly a project that one saves for his old age.

Actually I had expected finally to have some peace and quiet. The fact that I suddenly found myself facing this tremendous task was, as everybody knows, a shock for me. The responsibility is in fact enormous.

There was the moment when, as you later said, you felt just as if "a guillotine" were speeding down on you.

Yes, the thought of the guillotine occurred to me: Now it falls down and hits you. I had been so sure that this office was not my calling, but that God would now grant me some peace and quiet after strenuous years. But then I could only say, explain to myself: God's will is apparently otherwise, and something new and completely different is beginning for me. He will be with me.

In the so-called "room of tears" during a conclave three sets of robes lie waiting for the future Pope. One is long, one short, one middle-sized. What was going through your head in that room,

in which so many new Pontiffs are said to have broken down?
Does one wonder again here, at the very latest: Why me? What
does God want of me?

Actually at that moment one is first of all occupied by
very practical, external things. One has to see how to
deal with the robes and such. Moreover I knew that very
soon I would have to say a few words out on the balcony, and I began to think about what I could say. Besides,
even at the moment when it hit me, all I was able to say
to the Lord was simply: "What are you doing with me?
Now the responsibility is yours. You must lead me! I can't
do it. If you wanted me, then you must also help me!"
In this sense, I stood, let us say, in an urgent dialogue
relationship with the Lord: if he does the one thing he
must also do the other.

Did John Paul II want to have you as his successor?

That I do not know. I think he left it entirely up to the
dear Lord.

Nonetheless he did not allow you to leave office. That could be
taken as an argumentum e silentio, a silent argument for his
favorite candidate.

He did want to keep me in office; that is well known. As
my seventy-fifth birthday approached, which is the age
limit when one submits one's resignation, he said to me,
"You do not have to write the letter at all, for I want to
have you to the end." That was the great and undeserved
benevolence he showed me from the very beginning. He
had read my *Introduction to Christianity*. Evidently it was
an important book for him. As soon as he became Pope

he had made up his mind to call me to Rome as Prefect of the Congregation for the Doctrine of the Faith. He had placed a great, very cordial, and profound trust in me. As the guarantee, so to speak, that we would travel the right course in the faith.

You visited John Paul II one more time when he was on his death-bed. On that evening you hurried back from a lecture in Subiaco, where you had spoken about "Benedict's Europe in the Crisis of Cultures". What if anything did the dying Pope say to you?

He was suffering much and, nevertheless, very alert. He said nothing more, though. I asked him for his blessing, which he gave me. So we parted with a cordial hand-shake, conscious that that was our last meeting.

You did not want to become a bishop, you did not want to become Prefect, you did not want to become Pope. Isn't it fright-ening when things repeatedly happen quite against your own will?

It is like this: When a man says Yes during his priestly ordination, he may have some idea of what his own charism could be, but he also knows: I have placed myself into the hands of the bishop and ultimately of the Lord. I cannot pick and choose what I want. In the end I must allow myself to be led. I had in fact the notion that being a theology professor was my charism, and I was very happy when my idea became a reality. But it was also clear to me: I am always in the Lord's hands, and I must also be prepared for things that I do not want. In this sense it was certainly surprising suddenly to be snatched away and no longer to be able to follow my own path. But as I said, the fundamental Yes also contained the thought that I remain at the Lord's disposal and perhaps will also have to do things someday that I myself would not like.

You are now the most powerful Pope of all time. Never before has the Catholic Church had more believers, never before such extension, literally to the ends of the earth.

Naturally these statistics are important. They indicate how widespread the Church is and how large this communion is, which encompasses races and peoples, continents, cultures, and people of every kind. But the Pope does not have power because of these numbers.

Why not?

Communion with the Pope is something of a different sort, as is membership in the Church, of course. Among those 1.2 billion Catholics are many who inwardly are not there. Saint Augustine said even in his day: There are many outside who seem to be inside, and there are many inside who seem to be outside. In a matter like faith— like membership in the Catholic Church—inside and outside are mysteriously intertwined with each other. Stalin was right in saying that the Pope has no divisions and cannot issue commands. Nor does he have a big business in which all the faithful of the Church are his employees or his subordinates.

In that respect the Pope is, on the one hand, a completely powerless man. On the other hand, he bears a great responsibility. He is to a certain extent the leader, the representative, and at the same time the one responsible for making sure that the faith that keeps people together is believed, that it remains alive, and that its identity is inviolate. But only the Lord himself has the power to keep people in the faith as well.

For the Catholic Church the Pope is the Vicarius Christi, *Christ's representative on earth. Can you really speak for Jesus?*

In proclaiming the faith and in administering the sacraments every priest speaks on behalf of Jesus Christ, for Jesus Christ. Christ entrusted his Word to the Church. This Word lives in the Church. And if I accept interiorly the faith of this Church and live, speak and think on the basis of it, when I proclaim *Him*, then I speak for *Him*—even though of course there can always be shortcomings in the details. The important thing is that I do not present *my* ideas, but rather try to think and to live the Church's faith, to act in obedience to his mandate.

Is the Pope really "infallible", in the sense that the media sometimes bandy that term about? An absolute ruler whose thinking and will are law?

That is incorrect. The concept of infallibility developed over the course of centuries. It arose in view of the question of whether there is somewhere an ultimate authority that decides. The First Vatican Council, following a long tradition from the time of the early Christian community, finally determined that there is an ultimate decision! Everything does not remain open-ended! Under certain circumstances and under certain conditions the Pope can make final decisions that are binding, decisions that clarify what is and what is not the faith of the Church. This does not mean that the Pope can constantly issue "infallible" pronouncements. Usually the Bishop of Rome acts like any other bishop who professes his faith, who proclaims it, who is faithful in the Church. Only when certain conditions are present, when tradition has been clarified and he knows that he is not acting arbitrarily, can the Pope say: This is the faith of the Church—and denial of it is not the faith of the Church. In this sense the First Vatican Council defined the capability to make a final decision, so that the faith can maintain its binding authority.

The Petrine office, as you just explained, guarantees agreement with the truth and with authentic tradition. Communion with the Pope, then, is a prerequisite for right belief and freedom. Saint Augustine put it this way: Where Peter is, there is the Church, and there God is too. But this maxim originated in another time; it must no longer be valid today.

The saying was actually not formulated by Augustine nor in that way, but for our present purposes we can leave that open. In any case, it is an old axiom of the Catholic Church: Where Peter is, there is the Church. It goes without saying that the Pope can have private opinions that are wrong. But when he speaks, as we already said, as the supreme pastor of the Church, fully aware of his responsibility, then he no longer says something that is personally his, whatever happens to occur to him. Then, conscious of this great responsibility and at the same time of the Lord's protection, he knows that he is not misleading the Church in such a decision but, rather, is guaranteeing her unity with the past, the present, and the future and above all with the Lord. This is what it is about, and this is also what other Christian communities sense.

For a symposium on the occasion of the eightieth birthday of Paul VI you read a paper in 1977 about what a Pope should be and how he should act. He must "be the least one and conduct himself accordingly", as you quoted the English Cardinal Reginald Pole. He must profess "that he knows nothing but the one thing that was taught him by God the Father through Christ". The Vicar of Christ is one who keeps Christ's power present as a counterforce to the world's power. Not by any form of domination, but rather by carrying his superhuman burden on human shoulders. In this respect the real place of the Vicar of Christ is the cross.

Yes, I consider that correct even today. The primacy developed from the very beginning as a primacy of martyrdom. During the first three centuries Rome was the headquarters and capital of the Christian persecutions. Withstanding these persecutions and giving witness to Christ was the special task of the Roman episcopal see.

We can regard it as providential that at the moment when Christianity entered a period of peace with the State, the imperial throne was transferred to Constantinople on the Bosporus. Thus the Bishop of Rome could more easily set forth the independence of the Church, the fact that she is distinct from the State. We do not have to look deliberately for conflict, clearly, but rather should strive basically for consensus and understanding. Yet the Church, the Christian, and above all the Pope must always be prepared for the possibility that the witness he must give will become a scandal, will not be accepted, and that he will then be thrust into the situation of the Witness, the suffering Christ.

The fact that all the early Popes were martyrs is significant. Standing there as a glorious ruler is not part of being Pope, but rather giving witness to the One who was crucified and to the fact that he himself is ready also to exercise his office in this way, in union with him.

Of course there were also Popes who said to themselves: The Lord has given us the office, and now we wish to enjoy it, too.

Yes, that too is part of the mystery of papal history.

Christian willingness to be a sign of contradiction runs through your own biography like a continuous woven pattern. It begins in your parents' house, where resistance to an atheist system is understood as a hallmark of a Christian life. In the seminary you are helped by a rector who was detained in the Dachau concentration camp. As a priest you begin in a parish in Munich where both your predecessors were executed by the Nazis for fighting in the Resistance. During the Council you oppose the excessively narrow preliminary texts of the Church leadership. As a bishop you warn about the dangers of an affluent society. As a cardinal you fight against modification of core Christian doctrines by trends foreign to the faith.

Do these base lines now also influence the way in which you are shaping your pontificate?

Naturally the experience of so many years means also a formation of character; it leaves its mark on thought and action. I was, naturally, not always simply against things, exclusively and as a matter of principle. There were many wonderful situations of agreement. When I think of my time as an assistant pastor, even though the intrusion of the secular world was already perceptible in families, nevertheless there was so much joy in our common faith, in the school, with the children, with the youth, that I was really supported by that joy. And it was also like that at the time when I was a professor.

That Christianity gives joy and breadth is also a thread that runs through my whole life. Ultimately someone who is always only in opposition could probably not endure life at all.

But at the same time the fact was ever-present, albeit in varying doses, that the Gospel stands in opposition to powerful constellations. In my childhood and youth until the end of the war, of course, this was so in an especially drastic way. In the years after 1968,[1] the Christian faith then came into conflict with a new concept of society, so that it repeatedly had to stand against powerful, triumphal opinions. Enduring hostility and offering resistance are therefore part of it—a resistance, however, that serves to bring to light what is positive.

According to the Annuario Pontificio, the almanac of the Catholic Church, you erected in the year 2009 alone nine episcopal sees, an apostolic prefecture, two new metropolitan sees, and three apostolic vicariates. The number of Catholics increased by seventeen million, as many as the population of Greece and Switzerland combined. In the almost 3,000 dioceses you appointed 169 new bishops. Then there are all the audiences, the homilies, the journeys, the great number of decisions—and besides all that you also wrote a major study on Jesus, the second volume of which will be published in the near future. You are now eighty-three years old: Where do you get your energy?

First I must say that the statistics you list are a sign of the Church's vitality. Viewed exclusively from the European

[1] A year marked by upheavals in European universities.—Trans.

perspective, it appears that she is in decline. But that is only one part of the whole. In other parts of the world she is growing and thriving, she is quite dynamic. The number of new priests worldwide has increased in recent years, also the number of seminarians. We on the continent of Europe are experiencing only one particular side but not the great dynamic of a new beginning that is really present elsewhere and which I encounter again and again on my journeys and through the visits of the bishops.

You are right, though: that really overtaxes an eighty-three-year-old man. Thank God there are many good co-workers. Everything is developed and implemented in a common effort. I trust that our dear Lord will give me as much strength as I need to be able to do what is necessary. But I also notice that my forces are diminishing.

Nevertheless, one gets the impression that the Pope could teach a person something as a fitness trainer as well.

(Laughter.) I don't think so. Of course one must organize one's time correctly. And make sure that one gets enough rest. So that then one is suitably alert at the times when one is needed. In short: so that one follows the rhythm of the day in a disciplined way and knows when one will need energy.

Do you actually use the exercise bicycle that your former physician Dr. Buzzonetti set up for you?

No, I don't get to it at all—and don't need it at the moment, thank God.

So the Pope thinks like Churchill: "No sports!"

Yes!

From the Seconda Loggia, the reception chamber of the Apostolic Palace, you usually retire at six in the evening to your apartment so as to receive your most important collaborators in what you like to call your evening audiences. From 8:45 P.M. on, as a rule, the Pope has his privacy. What does a Pope do in his free time, assuming that he has any at all?

Yes, what does he do? Of course even in his free time he must study and read documents. There is always a great deal of work left over. But with the papal family, with the four women from the *Memores Domini* community and the two secretaries, there are meals in common, too; those are moments of relaxation.

Do you watch television together?

I watch the news with the secretaries, but sometimes we watch a DVD together as a group.

What films do you like?

There is a very beautiful film about Saint Josephine Bakhita, an African woman, which we watched recently. And then we like to watch Don Camillo and Peppone.[2]

By now you probably know the whole series by heart.

(Laughter.) Not quite.

---

[2] The pastor of a fictional Italian village and its Communist mayor, comic characters originally created by novelist Giovannino Guareschi in the 1950s.—TRANS.

So there are people who share in the Pope's private life, too.

Of course. We celebrate Christmas together, listen to the holiday music, and exchange gifts. The feast days of our patron saints are celebrated, and occasionally we also sing Evening Prayer together. So we celebrate feasts together. And then, besides our common meals, there is above all Holy Mass in common in the morning. That is an especially important moment in which we are all with each other in a particularly intense way in the light of the Lord.

The Pope is always dressed in white. Instead of a cassock does he sometimes wear a sweater in his free time?

No. That is a legacy left to me by the former second secretary of Pope John Paul II, Monsignor Mieczysław Mokrzycki, who told me: "The Pope *always* wore a cassock, and so must you."

The Romans were a little taken aback when they saw on the moving van the belongings with which you moved out of your residence into the Vatican after being elected the 264th successor of Peter. Did you furnish the papal appartamento with your used furniture?

My study at least. It was important for me to have my study the way it has developed over the course of many decades. In 1954 I bought my desk and the first bookshelves. Gradually there were additions. In them are all my advisors, the books; I know every nook and cranny, and everything has its history. Therefore I brought the whole study along with me. The other rooms were set up with the papal furniture.

Someone found out that you seem to be attached to perpetual timepieces. You wear a wristwatch from the sixties or seventies, a Junghans.

It belonged to my sister, who left it to me. When she died, the watch went to me.

A Pope does not even have his own briefcase, much less a salary. Is that right?

Yes, that is right.

Does he then at least get more help and consolation "from above" than, let's say, the average mortal?

Not only from above. I get so many letters from simple people, from religious sisters, from mothers, fathers, children, in which they encourage me. They write, "We pray for you, be not afraid, we like you." And they even enclose gifts of money and other little gifts....

The Pope receives monetary gifts?

Not for me personally, but so that I can help others with it. And I also find it very moving that simple people enclose something and tell me, "I know that you have to help so much, and I want to do a little, too." In this respect there are all kinds of consolations. And then there are the Wednesday audiences with the individual meetings. Letters arrive from old friends, occasionally visits, too, although of course that has become increasingly difficult. Since I always sense consolation "from above" as well and experience the nearness of the Lord while praying, and the beauty of the faith shines forth as I read the Church Fathers, there is a whole concert of consolations.

Has your faith changed since you have become responsible for Christ's flock as the supreme shepherd? Sometimes people get the impression that now it has become more mysterious somehow, more mystical.

I am no mystic. But it is correct that as Pope one has even more cause to pray and to entrust oneself entirely to God. For I see very well that almost everything I have to do is something I myself cannot do at all. That fact already forces me, so to speak, to place myself in the Lord's hands and to say to him: "You do it, if you want it!" In this sense prayer and contact with God are now even more necessary and also even more natural and self-evident than before.

To put it in worldly terms: Is there now a "better connection" to heaven, or something like a grace of office?

Yes, one often feels that. In the sense of: Now I have been able to do something that did not come from me at all. Now I entrust myself to the Lord and notice, yes, there is help there, something is being done that is not my own doing. In that sense there is absolutely an experience of the grace of office.

John Paul II once recounted that one day his father put a prayerbook with the "Prayer to the Holy Spirit" into his hands and told him that he should pray it daily. He then gradually understood what it means when Jesus says that the true worshippers of God are those who worship him "in spirit and truth". What does that mean?

This passage in chapter 4 of John's Gospel is the prophecy of a worship in which there will no longer be any temple, but in which the faithful will pray without an external temple in the fellowship of the Holy Spirit and the truth of the Gospel, in communion with Christ; where what is needed is no longer a visible temple but rather the new fellowship with the risen Lord. That always remains important, because it signifies a major turning point in the history of religion as well.

And how does Pope Benedict pray?

As far as the Pope is concerned, he too is a simple beggar before God—even more than all other people. Naturally I always pray first and foremost to our Lord, with whom I am united simply by old acquaintance, so to speak. But I also invoke the saints. I am friends with Augustine, with Bonaventure, with Thomas Aquinas. Then one says to such saints also: Help me! And the Mother of God is, in any case, always a major point of reference. In this sense I commend myself to the communion of saints. With them, strengthened by them, I then talk with the dear Lord also, begging, for the most part, but also in thanksgiving—or quite simply being joyful.

2. The Abuse Scandal

*The pontificate of Benedict XVI began with a wave of enthu-
siasm. Even the leader of the post-Communists in Italy was
complimentary: "His election is good news." According to Massimo
D'Alema, he is "sympathetic to people with intellect and culture". In his first year in office, the new Pope gathered almost
four million people on Saint Peter's Square, twice as many as
in the initial year of his predecessor. More than three million
copies of his first encyclical were sold in Italy alone. One million people flocked to the World Family Forum in Valencia,
Spain, to pray and celebrate together with the Pope. And the
popularity persisted. "Since the* Habemus Papam *on April 19
in Rome," the German news magazine* Der Spiegel *reported,
"the good will of the public toward Pope Benedict XVI, alias
Joseph Ratzinger, has continued."*

Did this success surprise you or perhaps even frighten you?

Yes, in one respect it did. But I knew: This does not come
from me. It became evident that the Church is alive. The
whole Church, indeed, you might say all mankind was
affected by the suffering of John Paul II and his death. We
all remember how Saint Peter's Square, how all of Rome
was full of people. That created to some extent a new awareness of the Pope and the Church, which obviously also
raised the question: Who is the new one? How can

18

anyone—after that great Pope—tackle the job in such a way that people will want to listen to him and get to know him?

Then, too, there is always the advance of something new, of a different style. In that respect I was grateful and happy that it kept going, that the approval remained. At the same time I was surprised that it was so great and so lively. But it was also clear to me that this comes from the inner continuity with the previous pontificate and from the abiding vitality of the Church.

For four years you are, as an ancient formula puts it, feliciter regnans, happily reigning. The new Pope enlarges the liturgical field by giving permission again for the Tridentine Mass. He announces within the framework of ecumenism the goal of complete unity with Orthodoxy—something to which the Church is closer now than she has been in a thousand years. He could be a member of the Green Party, given his position against war, injustice, and those who sin against the environment. He would fit in well with the leftists when he castigates "turbo-capitalism", the ever-increasing gap between the poor and the rich. One can sense a revitalization of the Church, a new self-assurance. And you succeed at something that no one thought possible after a giant like Wojtyła: a seamless transition of pontificates.

That was of course a gift. It helped that everyone knew that John Paul II liked me. That we had reached a deep spiritual understanding, and I realize also that in his regard I really am a debtor, a modest figure who is trying to continue what John Paul II accomplished as a giant.

Naturally, besides the things that arouse controversy and put us in the crossfire of criticism, there are always issues that the whole world has at heart and that are received positively by it.

My predecessor repeatedly met with great approval also as a great champion for human rights, peace, and freedom. These issues are still current. Today especially the Pope is obliged to stand up for human rights everywhere—as an intrinsic consequence of his belief that man is made in God's image and has a divine calling. He is obliged to fight for peace, against violence and threats of war. He has an inner obligation to struggle for the preservation of the environment and to oppose the destruction of creation.

So there are by nature many issues in which, so to speak, morality suits modernity. The modern world, after all, is not built solely out of the negative. If that were the case, it could not exist for long. It bears within itself great moral values, which also come precisely from Christianity, which through Christianity first emerged as values in the consciousness of mankind. Where they are supported—and they must be supported by the Pope—there is agreement in broad areas. We are happy about that. But that cannot blind us to the fact that there are other issues that cause controversy.

Eugen Biser, a liberal theologian at the University of Munich, already reckons you "among the most important Popes in history". With Benedict XVI, he says, a Church is beginning in which Christ "dwells in the hearts of men" through the invitation to experience God.

But suddenly the page turns. We recall your homily at your inauguration on April 24, 2005, in which you said, "Pray for me, that I may not flee for fear of the wolves." Had you suspected that this pontificate would also have very difficult stretches in store for you?

I had presumed that. But let me say first that one should always be very reticent about grading a Pope as important or unimportant during his lifetime. Only later do we see what rank something or someone assumes in history on the whole. But it was obvious, given our world situation with all its great forces of destruction, with the antagonisms that exist in it, the threats and errors, that there could not be cheerful approval all the time. If there had been nothing but approval, I would have had to ask myself seriously whether I was really proclaiming the whole Gospel.

The lifting of the excommunication of four bishops of the Society of Saint Pius X in January 2009 is an initial breach. We will come to speak about that later in detail, and also about the odd background of that case. All at once the man who previously was so highly praised that he was said to have actually started a "Benedetto fever" is now considered a "bad-luck Pope", someone who is alienating half the world. The commentaries are catastrophic. The Neue Zürcher Zeitung, *in view of an unprecedented anti-papal media campaign, feels obliged to speak about the "aggressive ignorance" of journalists. The Jewish French philosopher Bernard-Henri Lévy remarks that, as soon as the subject turns to Benedict XVI, "prejudices, dishonesty, and even outright disinformation dominate every discussion."*

Was the lifting of the excommunication a mistake?

Something ought to be said here perhaps about the lifting of the excommunication itself. For an incredible amount of nonsense was circulated, even by trained theologians. It is not true that those four bishops were excommunicated because of their negative attitude toward Vatican II, as was often supposed. In reality they were excommunicated because they had received episcopal ordination without a papal mandate. It was handled according to the applicable canon of the old canon law then in force. According to that canon, those who consecrate others as bishops without a papal mandate and also those who are thus consecrated are to be excommunicated. They were excommunicated, therefore, because they violated papal primacy. There is an analogous situation in China, where bishops were likewise consecrated without a papal mandate and hence were excommunicated. However: when such a bishop professes his acknowledgment both of the primacy in general and also that of the currently reigning Pope in particular, his excommunication is revoked, because there is no more reason for it. That is what we are doing in China—hoping thereby slowly to resolve the schism—and so we proceeded also in the cases concerned here. In short: for the sole reason that they had been consecrated without a papal mandate they were excommunicated; and for the sole reason that they now pronounced an acknowledgment of the Pope—albeit not yet following him on all points—their excommunication was revoked. That is per se quite a normal canonical procedure. Incidentally, I must say that in this matter our public relations work was a failure. It was not explained adequately why these bishops had been excommunicated and why they now, for purely canonical reasons, had to be absolved from the excommunication.

For the general public, there was the impression that Rome was dealing very leniently with right-wing, conservative groups, while left-wing and liberal activists were being quickly silenced.

In this case we were simply dealing with a clear, canonical situation. Vatican II was not involved at all. Nor the question of other theological positions. With their acknowledgment of the primacy of the Pope, these bishops, canonically speaking, had to be freed from the excommunication; this did not mean, however, that they had obtained any official ministries in the Church or that the position they had taken with regard to the Second Vatican Council had been accepted.

So "right-wing" and "left-wing" groups, let us say, are not being treated differently?

No. All are bound by the same canon law and by the same faith and have the same freedoms.

We will revisit the Williamson case in more detail later.
Exactly one year later, the darkest clouds gather over the Catholic Church. As though out of a deep abyss, countless incomprehensible cases of sexual abuse from the past come to light—acts committed by priests and religious. The clouds cast their shadows even on the Chair of Peter. Now no one is talking any more about the moral authority for the world that is usually granted a Pope. How great is this crisis? Is it really, as we occasionally read, one of the greatest in the history of the Church?

Yes, it is a great crisis, we have to say that. It was upsetting for all of us. Suddenly so much filth. It was really almost like the crater of a volcano, out of which suddenly a tremendous cloud of filth came, darkening and soiling everything, so that above all the priesthood suddenly seemed to be a place of shame and every priest was under the suspicion of being one like that too. Many priests declared that they no longer dared to extend a hand to a child, much less go to a summer camp with children.

For me the affair was not entirely unexpected. In the Congregation for the Doctrine of the Faith I had already dealt with the American cases; I had also seen the situation emerge in Ireland. But on this scale it was nevertheless an unprecedented shock. Since my election to the Chair of Peter I had already met several times with victims of sexual abuse. Three and a half years ago, in October 2006, in my address to the Bishops of Ireland, I had called for them to bring the truth to light, to take whatever steps necessary to prevent such egregious crimes from occurring again, to ensure that the principles of law and justice are fully respected and, above all, to bring healing to the victims. Suddenly to see the priesthood so defiled, and with it the Catholic Church herself, at the very heart—that was something that we were really just beginning to cope with. But it was imperative not to lose sight of the fact that there is good in the Church and not only those horrible things.

Cases of abuse in the Church are worse than elsewhere. Greater demands must be met by consecrated persons. Already at the beginning of the century, as you said, a series of abuse cases in the United States had become known. After the Ryan Report revealed the vast extent of sexual abuse in Ireland, too, the Church in another country was in shambles. "It will take generations", said the Irish religious priest Vincent Twomey, "to make reparation."

In Ireland the problem is altogether specific—there is a self-enclosed Catholic society, so to speak, which remained true to its faith despite centuries of oppression, but in which, then, evidently certain attitudes were also able to develop. I cannot analyze that in detail now. To see a country that gave the world so many missionaries, so many saints, which in the history of the missions also stands at the origin of our faith in Germany, now in a situation like this is tremendously upsetting and depressing. Above all, of course, for the Catholics in Ireland itself, where now as always there are many good priests. We must examine thoroughly how it was possible for that to happen, and at the same time what can be done so that something like that does not happen again.

You are right: It is a particularly serious sin when someone who is actually supposed to help people toward God, to whom a child or a young person is entrusted in order to find the Lord, abuses him instead and leads him away from the Lord. As a result the faith as such becomes unbelievable, and the Church can no longer present herself credibly as the herald of the Lord. All this shocked us and very deeply upsets me now as before. However, the Lord told us also that among the wheat there will be weeds—but that the seed, his seed, will nevertheless continue to grow. We are confident of that.

It is not only the abuse that is upsetting, it is also the way of dealing with it. The deeds themselves were hushed up and kept secret for decades. That is a declaration of bankruptcy for an institution that has love written on its banner.

The Archbishop of Dublin told me something very interesting about that. He said that ecclesiastical penal law functioned until the late 1950s; admittedly it was not perfect—there is much to criticize about it—but nevertheless it was applied. After the mid-sixties, however, it was simply not applied any more. The prevailing mentality was that the Church must not be a Church of laws but, rather, a Church of love; she must not punish. Thus the awareness that punishment can be an act of love ceased to exist. This led to an odd darkening of the mind, even in very good people.

Today we have to learn all over again that love for the sinner and love for the person who has been harmed are correctly balanced if I punish the sinner in the form that is possible and appropriate. In this respect there was in the past a change of mentality, in which the law and the need for punishment were obscured. Ultimately this also narrowed the concept of love, which in fact is not just being nice or courteous, but is found in the truth. And another component of truth is that I must punish the one who has sinned against real love.

In Germany the avalanche of discoveries of sexual abuse started because now the Church herself went public. A Jesuit preparatory school in Berlin reported the first cases, but very soon crimes from other institutions became known, and not only Catholic ones. But why were the revelations in America and Ireland not taken as the occasion to investigate immediately in other countries as well, to get in touch with victims—so as to eliminate any perpetrators who might still have been at work?

We responded to the matter in America immediately with revised, stricter norms. In addition, collaboration between the secular and ecclesiastical authorities was improved. Would it have been Rome's duty, then, to say to all the countries expressly: Find out whether you are in the same situation? Maybe we should have done that. For me, in any case, it was a surprise that abuse also existed on that scale in Germany.

The fact that newspapers and television reported extensively on such things was in the service of indispensable information. The ideologically tinged one-sidedness and aggressiveness of many in the media, however, took on the form of a propaganda war that exceeded all bounds. Regardless of that, the Pope made it clear: "The greatest persecution of the Church comes not from her enemies without, but arises from sin within the Church."

There was no overlooking the fact that what guided this press campaign was not only a sincere desire for truth, but there was also some pleasure in exposing the Church and if possible discrediting her. All that notwithstanding, one thing was always clear: Insofar as it is the truth, we must be grateful for every disclosure. The truth, combined with love rightly understood, is the number-one value. And finally, the media could not have reported in this way had there not been evil in the Church herself. Only because there was evil in the Church could it be played off against her by others.

Ernst-Wolfgang Böckenförde, a former German constitutional judge, remarked, "The words that Pope Benedict used years ago in the United States and now in his Letter to Irish Catholics could not be harsher." [1] *The real reason for the decades-long failure, he says, lies in deep-seated patterns of behavior according to a Church policy that places the welfare and reputation of the Church above all else. The welfare of the victims, on the other hand, automatically*

---

[1] See in the appendix the excerpts from the Pastoral Letter of Benedict XVI to the Irish Church, March 19th, 2010.

becomes a secondary matter, although actually they are first and
foremost the ones in need of the Church's protection.

Analyzing this is, of course, not easy. What does Church
policy mean? Why didn't people react formerly in the
same way they do now? Even the press formerly did not
take up such matters; the mentality back then was different. We know that the victims themselves, too, feel
great shame and do not necessarily want to be thrust
immediately into the spotlight. Many were able only
decades later to talk about what had happened to them.

It is important that we first take care of the victims
and do everything that we can to help, support, and heal
them; secondly that such acts be prevented by the proper
selection of candidates for the priesthood, as much as
possible; and thirdly that the perpetrators be punished
and be barred from any opportunity to repeat such acts.
To what extent the cases must then be made public is, I
think, a separate question, which will be answered differently in different stages of public awareness.

It is never permissible, however, to steal away and to
wish not to have seen it and to let the perpetrator continue working. It is therefore necessary for the Church
to be vigilant, to punish those who have sinned, and above
all to exclude them from further access to children. First
and foremost, as we said, comes charity toward the victims and efforts to do everything good to help them cope
with what they have experienced.

You had spoken on various occasions about instances of abuse,
last but not least in the Pastoral Letter to the Catholics of Ire-
land that was just mentioned. Nevertheless, there was an end-
less series of headlines like, "Pope Silent on Abuse Cases",

"Pope Wraps Himself in Silence", "Pope Benedict Silent on Abuse Scandals in the Catholic Church". Shouldn't some things have been said more often or louder in a world that has become so noisy and hard of hearing?

Of course one may wonder about that. Objectively, I think, everything essential was said. After all, what was true for Ireland was not said just to Ireland. To that extent the word of the Church and of the Pope was completely clear, unquestionable, and audible everywhere. In Germany, at first, we also had to leave it up to the bishops to speak. But one can always wonder whether the Pope should not speak more often. I would not venture to decide that now.

But ultimately you have to decide. Better communication might well have improved the situation.

Yes, that is right. But I think that, on the one hand, the essential thing really was said. And the fact that it applies not just to Ireland actually was clear. On the other hand, the bishops, as I already noted, have the first say. In that respect it was surely not wrong to wait.

The great majority of these cases took place decades ago. Nevertheless they burden your pontificate now in particular. Have you thought of resigning?

When the danger is great one must not run away. For that reason, now is certainly not the time to resign. Precisely at a time like this one must stand fast and endure the difficult situation. That is my view. One can resign at a peaceful moment or when one simply cannot go on. But one must not run away from danger and say that someone else should do it.

Is it possible then to imagine a situation in which you would consider a resignation by the Pope appropriate?

Yes. If a Pope clearly realizes that he is no longer physically, psychologically, and spiritually capable of handling the duties of his office, then he has a right and, under some circumstances, also an obligation to resign.

Anyone who followed the story in the mass media during those days must have had the impression that the Catholic Church is exclusively a system of injustice and sexual crimes. It was immediately said that Catholic teaching on sexuality and celibacy is directly connected with abuse. The fact that there were similar incidents in non-Catholic institutions faded into the background. The German criminologist Christian Pfeiffer reported that approximately 0.1 percent of those who committed abuse come from the personnel of the Catholic Church; 99.9 percent came from other areas. In the United States, a government report for the year 2008 lists the proportion of priests who were involved in cases of pedophilia at 0.03 percent. The Protestant Christian Science Monitor *published a study according to which the Protestant denominations in America are affected by a much higher rate of pedophilia.*

Is the Catholic Church being watched differently and evaluated differently with regard to abuse?

Actually you have already given the answer. If you look at the real statistics, that does not authorize us to look away from the problem or to minimize it. But we must also note that in these matters we are not dealing with something specific to the Catholic priesthood or the Catholic Church. They are, unfortunately, simply rooted in man's sinful situation, which is also present in the Catholic Church and led to these terrible results.

However, it is also important not to lose sight now of all the good that comes about through the Church. Not to ignore how many people are helped in their suffering, how many sick people, how many children are assisted, how much aid is provided. I think that whereas we must not minimize the evil and must sorrowfully acknowledge it, by the same token we must also still be grateful for how much light streams forth from the Catholic Church and should make that visible. It would lead to a collapse of entire sectors of social life if she were no longer there.

And nevertheless it is difficult for many people these days to stand by the Church. Can you understand why people respond by leaving in protest?

I can understand it. I am thinking of course above all about the victims themselves. That it is difficult for them to keep believing that the Church is a source of good, that she communicates the light of Christ, that she helps people in life—I can understand that. And others, who have only these negative perceptions, no longer see then the overall picture, the life of the Church. All the more reason that the Church must strive to make this vitality and greatness visible again, despite all that is negative.

As Prefect of the Congregation for the Doctrine of the Faith, immediately after the cases of abuse in the United States became known, you issued guidelines for dealing with those cases. They also deal with cooperation with the civil authorities and ongoing preventive measures. This should forestall any cover-ups. The guidelines were made even stricter in 2003. What conclusions does the Vatican draw from cases that have recently become known?

These guidelines have now been newly revised once more and were recently published in the final version. Always as a continuation of the experience that has been gained, so as to be able to respond better, more precisely and correctly to this situation. Yet penal law alone is not sufficient here. It is one thing to handle these cases in a way that is legally correct. It is another thing to ensure as much as possible that they no longer happen. To that end we authorized a major visitation of the seminaries in America. Here there were evidently also instances of neglect, failure to investigate carefully enough young men who did have a special gift for working with youth and seemed also to be religiously inclined, but who should have been recognized as being unsuited for the priesthood. Prevention is therefore an important field. Then there is the need for positive formation in true chastity and in dealing correctly with one's own sexuality and that of others. Then theologically as well there is certainly much to be developed and an appropriate climate to be created. And then of course the whole faith community should also become involved in thinking about vocations and promoting them and being attentive to individuals. On the one hand, to guide and support them—and, on the other hand, to help the superiors discern whether or not persons are suitable. And so there must be a whole bundle of measures—on the one hand, preventive, on the other hand, reactive—and finally, positive measures in creating a spiritual climate in which these things can be eliminated, overcome, and as far as possible precluded.

Recently in Malta you met with several victims of abuse. One of them, Joseph Magro, said afterward, "The Pope wept along with me, although he is in no way guilty for what happened to me." What were you able to say to the victims?

Actually I could not say anything special at all to them. I was able to tell them that it affects me very deeply. That I suffer with them. And that was not just an expression, but it really touches my heart. And I was able to tell them that the Church will do everything possible so that this does not happen again, and that we intend to help them as well as we can. And finally, that we keep them in our prayers and ask them not to lose faith in Christ as the true light and in the living communion of the Church.

3. Causes of the Crisis and a New Opportunity

You pronounced an unforgettable indictment during the Stations of the Cross on Good Friday of 2005, a few weeks before you were elected the successor of John Paul II: "How often do we celebrate only ourselves, without even realizing that he is there! How often is his Word twisted and misused!" And as though aimed at the events of the near future: "How much filth there is in the Church, and even among those who, in the priesthood, ought to belong entirely to him!"

Now, right during the Year for Priests that you proclaimed, all of these failures and crimes come to light. From a biblical perspective, should not the revelation of these scandals itself perhaps be taken as a sign?

One might think that the devil could not stand the Year for Priests and therefore threw this filth in our faces. As it wanted to show the world how much filth there was, even and precisely among priests. On the other hand, one could say that the Lord wanted to test us and to call us to a deeper purification, so that we would not celebrate the Year for Priests in a triumphalist way, as self-glorification, but rather as a year of purification, of interior renewal, transformation, and above all penance.

34

The concept of penance, which is one of the fundamental elements of the Old Testament message, is something we have increasingly lost. People somehow wanted to say only positive things. But the negative things do exist; that is a fact. The fact that one can change and allow oneself to be changed through penance is a positive gift. The early Church viewed it in this way also. It is imperative now really to start over in the spirit of penance—and at the same time not to lose our joy in the priesthood but to recover it again.

And I can say with great gratitude: this is what happened, too. I have received from bishops, priests, and lay people many deeply moving testimonials of gratitude for the Year for Priests, which touch the heart. These people testify: We understood the Year for Priests as an occasion for purification, as an act of humility, in which we allow ourselves to be called by the Lord again. And precisely thereby we have also seen the greatness and beauty of the priesthood. In this sense, I think, these horrible revelations were after all an act of providence as well, which humbles us and forces us to begin over again.

The causes of abuse are complex. Aghast, one wonders most of all how someone who reads the Gospel every day and celebrates Holy Mass, who is constantly exposed to the sacraments and is actually supposed to be strengthened by them, can go astray in this horrible way.

That is a question that really touches on the *mysterium iniquitatis*, the mystery of evil. One wonders also in this regard: What does someone like that think in the morning when he goes to the altar and offers the Holy Sacrifice? Does he actually go to confession? What does he say in confession? What consequences does that confession have for him? It really ought to be the major factor in extricating him from it and compelling him to amend his life. It is a mystery that someone who has pledged himself to what is holy can lose it so completely and then, indeed, can lose his origins. At his priestly ordination he must have had at least a longing for what is great and pure; otherwise he would not have made that choice. How can someone then fall so far?

We do not know. But this means all the more that priests must support one another and must not lose sight of one another. That bishops are responsible for this and that we must beg the lay faithful also to help support their priests. And I see in the parishes that love for the priest grows when they recognize his weaknesses and take it upon themselves to help him in those weaknesses.

Maybe some of us, too, have a completely wrong image of the Church. As though she could be free of such things and as though she were not susceptible to temptations, too—she especially. Allow me to quote once again from your meditations on the Way of the Cross: "The soiled garments and face of your Church throw us into confusion. Yet it is we ourselves who have soiled them!... When we fall, we drag you down to earth, and Satan laughs, for he hopes that you will not be able to rise from that fall; he hopes that being dragged down in the fall of your Church, you will remain prostrate and overpowered."

Yes, that is what we can see today with our own eyes and what comes forcibly to mind, especially in meditating on the Way of the Cross. Here it becomes clear that Christ did not suffer because of some accident or another, but really took the whole history of mankind into his own hands. His suffering for us is not merely a theological formula. To see this and then to let ourselves be drawn by him to *his* side, and not to the other side, is an existential act. In meditating on the Way of the Cross we realize: He is really suffering for us. And he also took upon himself *my* cause. Now he is drawing me to himself by seeking me out in the depths of myself and bringing me back up to himself.

Evil, too, will always be part of the mystery of the Church. And when we see what men, what the clergy have done in the Church, then that is nothing short of proof that he founded and upholds the Church. If she were dependent on men, she would long since have perished.

The great majority of abuse cases go back to the 1970s and 1980s. For this reason the Prefect of the Congregation for Institutes of Consecrated Life, Cardinal Franc Rodé, referred in this context also to the decline in faith over many years and the undermining of the Church that were additional causes of the scandal. "Secularized culture has penetrated into some Western religious orders," Rodé says, "and yet religious life is supposed to be precisely an alternative to the 'dominant culture' instead of reflecting it."

Of course the intellectual climate of the 1970s, for which the 1950s had already paved the way, contributed to this. A theory was even finally developed at that time that pedophilia should be viewed as something positive. Above all, however, the thesis was advocated—and this even infiltrated Catholic moral theology—that there was no such thing as something that is bad in itself. There were only things that were "relatively" bad. What was good or bad depended on the consequences.

In such a context, where everything is relative and nothing intrinsically evil exists, but only relative good and relative evil, people who have an inclination to such behavior are left with no solid footing. Of course pedophilia is first rather a sickness of individuals, but the fact that it could become so active and so widespread was linked also to an intellectual climate through which the foundations of moral theology, good and evil, became open to question in the Church. Good and evil became interchangeable; they were no longer absolutely clear opposites.

The Church was shaken also by revelations about the double life of Marcial Maciel Degollado, the founder of a religious congregation of priests, the Legion of Christ. Sexual abuse accusations against Maciel, who died in 2008 in the United States, had already been in place for years. Maciel's partner stated that she is the mother of two of his children. Some voices in Mexico now are claiming that the public apologies of the Legionaries of Christ are not sufficient, that the congregation must be dissolved.

Unfortunately we addressed these things very slowly and late. Somehow they were concealed very well, and only around the year 2000 did we have any concrete clues. Ultimately unequivocal evidence was needed in order to be sure that the accusations were grounded. To me Marcial Maciel remains a mysterious figure. There is, on the one hand, a life that, as we now know, was out of moral bounds—an adventurous, wasted, twisted life. On the other hand, we see the dynamism and the strength with which he built up the congregation of Legionaries.

Meanwhile we have had an Apostolic Visitation carried out and appointed a delegate who together with a group of collaborators is preparing the necessary reforms. Naturally corrections must be made, but by and large the congregation is sound. In it there are many young men who enthusiastically want to serve the faith. This enthusiasm must not be destroyed. Many of them have been called by a false figure to what is, in the end, right after all. That is the remarkable thing, the paradox, that a false prophet, so to speak, could still have a positive effect. New courage must be given to these numerous young men. A new structure is needed so that they do not fall between the cracks but are guided correctly so as to be able to continue performing a service to the Church and to mankind.

The case of Maciel is unique, but in addition there are priests everywhere who either secretly or else with the knowledge of their religious community or even of the Church authorities are living in a quasi-marital relationship. The scandal becomes that much the worse when children from those unions end up in orphanages while the Church pays for their support.

That should not be. Anything involving lies and concealment should not be. Again and again in the history of the Church, unfortunately, there are times when such situations occur and spread, especially when they lie, so to speak, within the trend of the spiritual climate of the time. This is of course also an especially urgent challenge for us all. When a priest lives together with a woman, one must examine whether a real will to marry is present and whether they could build a good marriage. If that is the case, they must follow that path. If it is a question of a failure of moral will, but no real interior union is there, one must try to find paths of healing for him and for her. In any case care should be taken that justice is done for the children—they are the primary good—and that they obtain the living and educational surroundings they need.

The fundamental problem is honesty. The second problem is respect for the truth of the two individuals and of the children, so as to find the right solution. The third is: How can we again raise young men for celibacy? How can we support the priests who live it out in such a way that it remains a sign in these confused times, in which not only celibacy but also marriage is seriously in crisis? Many claim that there is no such thing as monogamous marriage any more. It is an enormous challenge to support and develop both of them anew, celibacy and marriage. Monogamous marriage is part of the foundation on which Western civilization is based. If it collapses, something essential to the essence of our culture collapses.

The scandal of sexual abuse could cause us to ask about other cases of abuse as well. For instance, the abuse of power. The abuse of a relationship. The abuse of a commission to educate. The misuse of my gifts. In ancient Greece a tragedy was supposed to cause strong emotions in the spectators, a "cathartic" or cleansing effect that made them think in a new way about their life. Only catharsis makes people ready to change their deeply ingrained behaviors. Couldn't the current crisis of the Church become a new opportunity also?

I think so. Indeed, I have already mentioned that the Year for Priests, which turned out quite differently from what we had expected, had a cathartic effect also. That the laity, too, became grateful again for what the priesthood really is and saw its positive nature in a new way, precisely in the midst of the disturbances and the threats to it.

This catharsis is for all of us, for all of society, but especially of course for the Church, a call to recognize again our fundamental values and to see the dangers that profoundly threaten not only priests but also society as a whole. Knowledge about this threat and the destruction of the moral framework of our society should be for us a call to purification. We must acknowledge again that we cannot simply live in any way we please. That freedom cannot be arbitrariness. That it is imperative to learn to exercise a freedom that is responsibility.

4. The Global Catastrophe

The crisis in the Church is one thing; the crisis of secularism is another. The one crisis may be serious, but the other increasingly resembles a permanent global catastrophe. Because of climate change, the tropics are expanding, the sea level is rising. The poles are melting; holes in the ozone layer are no longer closing up. We are experiencing tragedies like the oil disaster in the Gulf of Mexico, gigantic wildfires, unprecedented catastrophic floods, unexpected heat waves and periods of drought.

The General Secretary of the United Nations, Ban Ki-Moon, as early as November 2007, described the condition of planet earth before the UN Assembly in New York as "extremely at risk". A UN investigatory commission determined that only a few decades remain for mankind until a point of no return— where it is too late to gain control of the problem of the high-tech world on our own. Some experts from various fields even consider that we have already reached this point.

"God saw everything that he had made," the Book of Genesis says, "and behold, it was very good." It is frightening, then, what has meanwhile become of this dream of a planet. The question is this: Is the earth quite simply not sustaining the enormous developmental potential of our species? Is it perhaps not designed at all for us to remain here in the long run? Or are we doing something wrong here?

Sacred Scripture tells us, and experience too tells us, that we do not remain here forever. But surely we are doing something wrong. I think that the problematic nature of the concept of progress has some bearing on it. The modern era has tried to find its way according to the fundamental concepts of progress and freedom. But what is progress? Today we see that progress can also be destructive. In this regard we should reflect on what criteria we must find so that progress really is progress.

The concept of progress originally had two aspects: On the one hand, there was progress in knowledge. People understood this to mean comprehending reality. That has also happened to an incredible extent through the combination of the mathematical world view and experimentation. As a result, today we can reconstruct DNA, the structure of life, and in general the functional structure of all reality—to the point where by now we can partially copy it and already begin to manufacture life ourselves. In this respect new possibilities for man have also come about with this progress.

The basic idea was: progress is knowledge.

And knowledge is power. That means: if I know, then I can also control. Knowledge brought power, but in such a way that with our own power we can now also destroy the world that we think we have figured out intellectually.

So it becomes apparent that in the previous concept of progress, compounded of knowledge and power, an essential perspective is lacking, namely, the aspect of the good. This is the question: What is good? Where should knowledge lead power? Is it just a matter of being able to control in general—or must we also ask the question about the intrinsic standards, about what is good for man and for the world? And this, I think, has not happened in an adequate way. As a result the ethical aspect, of which responsibility in the sight of the Creator is a basic part, has essentially to a great extent been left out. Then, when one's own power is the only thing being advanced by one's knowledge, this sort of progress becomes really destructive.

What consequences should follow now?

A major examination of conscience should begin today. What really is progress? Is it progress if I can destroy? Is it progress if I myself can make, select, and dispose of human beings? How can progress be achieved ethically and humanely? But not only the criteria for progress would have to be reconsidered. Besides knowledge and progress, it is also a question of the other fundamental concept of the modern era: freedom, which is understood as the freedom to be able to do anything.

This sort of thinking results in the claim that science is indivisible. This means that whatever one can do, one must also be allowed to do. Anything else would be contrary to freedom. Is that true? I think that it is not true. We see how enormously man's power has grown. But what did not grow along with it was his ethical potential. This imbalance is reflected today in the products of a progress that was not considered in moral terms. Now the big question is: How can we correct the concept and reality of progress and then also master it in a positive way from within? In this regard a comprehensive reexamination of basic principles is necessary.

How difficult it is for us to change these criteria of progress was made clear by the World Climate Conference in Copenhagen in December 2009. It had taken seventeen years for the governments of the world to get from the first meeting in Rio to this decisive summit meeting, which scientists, environmentalists, and politicians have declared to be one of the most important conferences in the history of mankind. The basis for it was the research finding of more than a thousand scientists, who on behalf of the UN's Intergovernmental Panel on Climate Control (IPCC) calculated that global temperatures from now on should be allowed to increase by at most two degrees Centigrade [3.6 degrees Fahrenheit]. Any further warming would push the climate irreversibly beyond a tipping point. The compromise draft document from Copenhagen, however, does not even include concrete goals. The two-degree limit will now be surpassed with a high degree of certainty. The consequences of that are storms, floods, and parched harvests. Doesn't this outcome necessarily confirm that mankind is altogether incapable of ever resolving a threat such as climate change in a collective effort?

That is in fact the big problem. What can we do? Meanwhile, in view of the threatening catastrophe, there is the recognition everywhere that we must make moral decisions. There is also a more or less pronounced awareness of a global responsibility for it; that ethics must no longer refer merely to one's own group or one's own nation, but rather must keep the earth and all people in view.

To this extent a certain potential for moral insight is present. But the conversion of this into political will and political actions is then rendered largely impossible by the lack of willingness to do without. After all, this would have to be implemented in national budgets and finally carried out by individuals, which then in turn leads to an unequal burdening of various groups.

So it becomes clear that the political will ultimately cannot become effective unless there is in all mankind—especially on the part of the chief supporters of development and progress—a new, deeper moral awareness, a willingness to do without, which is concrete and which for the individual also becomes an acknowledged value for his life.

The question is therefore: How can the great moral will, which everybody affirms and everyone invokes, become a personal decision? For unless that happens, politics remains impotent. Who, therefore, can ensure that this general awareness also penetrates the personal sphere? This can be done only by an authority that touches the conscience, that is close to the individual and does not merely call for eye-catching events.

In that respect this is a challenge for the Church. She not only has a major responsibility; she is, I would say, often the only hope. For she is so close to people's consciences that she can move them to particular acts of self-denial and can inculcate basic attitudes in souls.

The philosopher Peter Sloterdijk says concerning global geo-management, "People are atheists about the future. They do not believe what they know, even when someone cogently proves to them what has to come."

Maybe they do believe it theoretically. But they tell themselves that it will not affect me. In any case I will not change *my* life. And then finally there are not only individual egotisms opposed to each other, but also group egotisms. People are accustomed to a particular sort of life, and when this is threatened, they of course put up resistance. Then again, one sees too few models of what self-denial could look like concretely. In this respect the religious communities are important as examples. They can in their own way demonstrate that a life-style of reasonable, moral self-denial is quite practicable, without having to exclude entirely the possibilities of our time.

If it is a question of a good example, the State has not proved to be very exemplary either. Governments today pile up debts to heights never seen before. A single country like Germany spent no less than 43.9 billion Euros just on interest payments to banks; in other words, for the fact that despite all our wealth we have lived beyond our means. Those interest payments alone would be enough to provide food for a year for all the children in developing countries. Worldwide, since the onset of the financial crisis, government debt has increased by 45 percent—by now totaling more than 50 trillion dollars—inconceivable figures, and a completely unprecedented situation. In 2010 the member states of the European Union alone are taking out more than 800 billion Euros of new loans. The new debt in the United States government budget is pegged at 1.56 trillion dollars, the high point of all time. The Harvard Professor Kenneth Rogoff says, therefore, that there is no normality any more, but only an illusion of normality. Certainly generations to come are being burdened with colossal debts. Isn't that also an insanely big moral problem?

Naturally, because we are living at the expense of future generations. In this respect it is plain that we are living in untruth. We live on the basis of appearances, and the huge debts are meanwhile treated as something that we are simply entitled to. Here, too, everyone understands in theory that it would require careful deliberation to recognize again what is really possible, what one can do, and what one may do. And yet people do not take it to heart.

Above and beyond the individual financial plans, a global examination of conscience is indispensable. The Church has tried to make a contribution in this regard with the encyclical *Caritas in veritate*. It does not give answers that would solve everything. But it is a step toward putting things into another perspective and looking at them not only from the point of view of feasibility and success, but from the point of view that sees love of neighbor as something normative and is oriented to God's will and not just to our desires. In this respect impetus would have to be provided in this way so that a change of consciousness can really come about.

We have acknowledged the problem of environmental destruction. However, the fact that saving our spiritual ozone layer and especially saving our spiritual rainforests is the prerequisite for saving the ecology seems to penetrate our consciousness only very slowly. Shouldn't we have asked long ago: What about the contamination of our thinking, the pollution of our souls? Many things that we permit in this media- and commerce-driven society are basically the equivalent of a toxic load that almost inevitably must lead to a spiritual poisoning.

There is no overlooking the fact that there is a poisoning of thought, which in advance leads us into false perspectives. To free ourselves again from it by means of a real conversion—to use that fundamental word of the Christian faith—is one of the challenges that by now are becoming obvious to everyone. In our modern world, which is so scientifically oriented, such concepts no longer had any meaning. A conversion, as faith understands it, toward the will of God who shows us a way was considered old-fashioned and outmoded. I believe, though, that gradually it is becoming evident that there is something to it when we say that we must reconsider all this.

The abbess and physician Hildegard von Bingen summed up these considerations over nine hundred years ago in the following formula: "When man sins, the cosmos suffers." The problems of the current hour in history, you write in your book on Jesus, are the consequences of the fact that people no longer listen to God. In another place you even speak about the "obscuring" of the light that comes from God.

For many people today, practical atheism is the normal rule of life. Maybe there is something or someone, they think, who once set the world in motion eons ago, but he does not matter to us at all. If this attitude becomes a general existential position, then freedom no longer has any standards, then everything is possible and permissible. That is why it is so urgent also to bring the question about God back into the center. Of course, this does not mean a God who exists in some way or other, but rather a God who knows us, speaks to us, and approaches us—and who is then our judge also.

5. Dictatorship of Relativism

In his futuristic novel Brave New World, the British author Aldous Huxley had predicted in 1932 that falsification would be the decisive element of modernity. In a false reality with its false truth—or the absence of truth altogether—nothing, in the final analysis, is important any more. There is no truth, there is no standpoint. Today, in fact, truth is regarded as far too subjective a concept for us to find therein a universally valid standard. The distinction between genuine and fake seems to have been abolished. Everything is to some extent negotiable. Is that the relativism against which you were warning so urgently?

It is obvious that the concept of truth has become suspect. Of course it is correct that it has been much abused. Intolerance and cruelty have occurred in the name of truth. To that extent people are afraid when someone says, "This is the truth", or even "I have the truth." We never have it; at best it has us. No one will dispute that one must be careful and cautious in claiming the truth. But simply to dismiss it as unattainable is really destructive.

A large proportion of contemporary philosophies, in fact, consist of saying that man is not capable of truth. But viewed in that way, man would not be capable of ethical values, either. Then he would have no standards. Then he would only have to consider how he arranged things reasonably for himself, and then at any rate the opinion of the majority would be the only criterion that counted. History, however, has sufficiently demonstrated how destructive majorities can be, for instance, in systems such as Nazism and Marxism, all of which also stood against truth in particular.

"We are building a dictatorship of relativism", you declared in your homily at the opening of the conclave [in 2005], "that does not recognize anything as definitive and whose ultimate standard consists solely of one's own ego and desires."

That is why we must have the courage to dare to say: Yes, man must seek the truth; he is capable of truth. It goes without saying that truth requires criteria for verification and falsification. It must always be accompanied by tolerance, also. But then truth also points out to us those constant values which have made mankind great. That is why the humility to recognize the truth and to accept it as a standard has to be relearned and practiced again.

The truth comes to rule, not through violence, but rather through its own power; this is the central theme of John's Gospel: When brought before Pilate, Jesus professes that he himself is The Truth and the witness to the truth. He does not defend the truth with legions but rather makes it visible through his Passion and thereby also implements it.

In a world that has become relativistic, a new paganism has gained more and more dominion over people's thoughts and actions. It has long since become clear not only that there is a blank space, a vacuum, alongside the Church, but also that something like an anti-church has been established. The Pope in Rome, one German newspaper wrote, should be condemned for the sole reason that by his positions he has "transgressed against the religion" that today "is valid in this country", namely, the "civil religion". Has a new Kulturkampf *started here, as Marcello Pera has analyzed it? The former president of the Italian Senate speaks about a "large-scale battle of secularism against Christianity".*

A new intolerance is spreading, that is quite obvious. There are well-established standards of thinking that are supposed to be imposed on everyone. These are then announced in terms of so-called "negative tolerance". For instance, when people say that for the sake of negative tolerance [i.e. "not offending anyone"] there must be no crucifix in public buildings. With that we are basically experiencing the abolition of tolerance, for it means, after all, that religion, that the Christian faith is no longer allowed to express itself visibly.

When, for example, in the name of non-discrimination, people try to force the Catholic Church to change her position on homosexuality or the ordination of women, then that means that she is no longer allowed to live out her own identity and that, instead, an abstract, negative religion is being made into a tyrannical standard that everyone must follow. That is then seemingly freedom—for the sole reason that it is liberation from the previous situation.

In reality, however, this development increasingly leads to an intolerant claim of a new religion, which pretends to be generally valid because it is reasonable, indeed, because it is reason itself, which knows all and, therefore, defines the frame of reference that is now supposed to apply to everyone.

In the name of tolerance, tolerance is being abolished; this is a real threat we face. The danger is that reason—so-called Western reason—claims that it has now really recognized what is right and thus makes a claim to totality that is inimical to freedom. I believe that we must very emphatically delineate this danger. No one is forced to be a Christian. But no one should be forced to live according to the "new religion" as though it alone were definitive and obligatory for all mankind.

The aggressiveness with which this new religion appears was described by the weekly news magazine Der Spiegel *as a "crusade of the atheists". It is a crusade that mocks Christianity as the "God delusion" and classifies religion as a curse that is also to blame for all wars.*

You yourself have already spoken about a "subtle or even not so subtle aggression against the Church". Even without a totalitarian regime, you say that there is pressure today to think the way everybody thinks, that attacks against the Church show "how this conformity can really be a genuine dictatorship". Harsh words.

But the reality is in fact such that certain forms of behavior and thinking are being presented as the only reasonable ones and, therefore, as the only appropriately human ones. Christianity finds itself exposed now to an intolerant pressure that at first ridicules it—as belonging to a perverse, false way of thinking—and then tries to deprive it of breathing space in the name of an ostensible rationality.

It is very important for us to oppose such a claim of absoluteness conceived as a certain sort of "rationality". Indeed, this is not pure reason itself but rather the restriction of reason to what can be known scientifically—and at the same time the exclusion of all that goes beyond it. Of course it is true that historically there have been wars because of religion, too, that religion has also led to violence. . . .

But neither Napoleon nor Hitler nor the U.S. Army in Vietnam had anything to do with wars of religion. On the contrary, exactly seventy years ago atheistic systems in the East and the West reduced the world to ruins, in an epoch distanced from God that the American writer Louis Begley called "a satanic requiem".

It is all the more true that there is still the great power of good, also, which was delivered by religion and is present and resplendent throughout history—think of great names such as Francis of Assisi, Vincent de Paul, Mother Teresa, and so on. Conversely, the new ideologies have led to a sort of cruelty and contempt for mankind that was hitherto unthinkable, because there was still respect for God's image, whereas without this respect man makes himself absolute and is allowed to do anything—and then really becomes a destroyer.

On the other hand, one could say that a State, with a view to the equality of all, must also have the right to banish religious symbols from the public square, even the Cross of Christ. Is that understandable?

Here we must first ask the question: Why must the State banish it? If the Cross contained a message that was not comprehensible or acceptable to others, then that would surely be worth considering. But the Cross contains the message that God himself is someone who suffers, that through suffering he is fond of us, that he loves us. This is a message that attacks no one. That is the one thing.

On the other hand, there is of course also a cultural identity on which our countries are based. An identity that positively shapes our countries and supports them from within—and that continues to form positive values and the basic structure of society, through which egotism is kept within its limits and a humane culture is possible. I would say that such a cultural self-expression of a society, which lives *in a positive way* as a result of it, cannot offend anyone who does not share this conviction, and it must not be banned either.

In Switzerland the citizens voted, not against the construction of mosques, but against the construction of minarets at mosques. In France the Parliament has forbidden wearing the burqa. Can Christians be glad about that?

Christians are tolerant, and in that respect they also allow others to have their self-image. We are grateful that in the countries along the Persian Gulf (Qatar, Abu Dhabi, Dubai, Kuwait) there are churches in which Christians can worship, and we wish it to be like this everywhere. For this reason it goes without saying that Muslims in our countries can also gather in mosques for prayer. As for the burqa, I see no reason for a general ban. Some say that many women would not wear the burqa voluntarily at all and that it is actually a violation of women. One can, of course, not agree to that. But if they want to wear it voluntarily, I do not know why it must be prohibited.

In Italy 80 percent of the inhabitants are baptized Catholics. In Portugal it is 90 percent, and in Poland likewise 90 percent, and in little Malta 100 percent. In Germany more than 60 percent of the population still belongs to the two Christian state churches, and a considerable portion to other Christian communities as well. Western Christian culture is no doubt the basis for the success and prosperity of Europe—and yet today a majority allows itself to be dominated by a minority that shapes public opinion. A remarkable if not actually schizophrenic situation.

We see in this an intrinsic problem. For to what extent do people still belong to the Church in the first place? On the one hand, they want to belong to her and do not want to lose this foundation. On the other hand, they are of course also shaped and formed interiorly by the modern way of thinking. It is the unfermented coexistence, with and alongside each other, of the basic Christian intention and a new world view, which leaves its mark on all of life. To that extent what remains is a sort of schizophrenia, a divided existence.

We must strive to integrate the two, insofar as they are compatible with each other. Being Christian must not become a sort of archaic stratum to which I cling somehow and on which I live to a certain extent *alongside* of modernity. Christianity is itself something living, something modern, which thoroughly shapes and forms all of my modernity—and in this sense actually embraces it.

That a major spiritual effort is required here I expressed most recently by founding a "Pontifical Council for Promoting the New Evangelization". It is important for us to try to live Christianity and to think as Christians in such a way that it incorporates what is good and right about modernity—and at the same time separates and distinguishes itself from what is becoming a counter-religion.

Viewed objectively, the Catholic Church is the largest organiza-
tion in the world, with a smooth-running, centrally organized net-
work extending over the entire globe. She has 1.2 billion members;
she has 4,000 bishops, 400,000 priests, and millions of religious.
She has thousands of universities, monasteries and convents, schools
and social institutions. In countries like Germany, she is the larg-
est employer after the government. She is not just a premium brand
with inviolable principles, but has her own identity; with her own
worship, her own ethics, with the most holy of all things holy, the
Eucharist. And in the first place: she has her legitimacy from "on
high" and can say of herself: We are the original, and we are the
guardians of the treasure. It doesn't get any better than this. Isn't
it strange, or even a scandal, that this Church does not make far
more out of this incomparable potential?

Of course we have to ask ourselves that. It is the clash of
two spiritual worlds, the world of faith and the world of
secularism. The question is: Where is secularism right?
Where can and must the faith adopt the forms and figures of modernity—and where must it offer resistance?
This great struggle pervades the whole world today. The
bishops in the Third World countries tell me: We, too,
have secularism at home; there it still coincides entirely
with archaic ways of life.

   Really, one often wonders how it happens that Christians who personally are believers do not have the strength
to put their faith into action in a way that is politically
more effective. Above all else we must try to make sure
that people do not lose sight of God. That they recognize the treasure they have. And that they themselves,
then, as a result of the strength of their own faith, enter
into the conflict with secularism and are capable of carrying out the discernment of spirits. This tremendous

process is the real, great task of this hour. We can only hope that the inner strength of the faith that is present in people will then become powerful publicly as well by leaving its imprint on public thinking, too, and that society does not simply fall into the abyss.

Couldn't we also assume that after two thousand years Christianity has simply played itself out, just as other major cultures in the history of civilization played themselves out?

If we look superficially and have only the Western world in view, then we might think that. But if we look more closely, as it is possible for me to do precisely because of the visits of bishops from all over the world and many other encounters, we see that at this hour Christianity is developing a new creativity at the same time.

In Brazil, for example, there is, on the one hand, strong growth among the sects, which are often very dubious because, for the most part, they promise only prosperity, external success. There are also, however, new Catholic awakenings, a dynamic of new movements, for instance, the "Heralds of the Gospel", young people who are seized by the enthusiasm of having acknowledged Christ as the Son of God and of bringing him into the world. As the Archbishop of São Paolo tells me, new movements are being formed there constantly. And so there is a force of new life and awakening there.

Or we could think of what the Church means for Africa. There, in the confusion and destruction of wars, she is often the only thing that always remains; the only refuge where there is still humanity; where something is being done for people. She is committed to the proposition that life can go on, that there can be care for the sick, that children can come into the world and be raised. She is a vital force that again and again creates new enthusiasm and then develops new ways.

Less clearly but nevertheless unmistakably, we find here in the West, too, a revival of new Catholic initiatives that are not ordered by a structure or a bureaucracy. The bureaucracy is spent and tired. These initiatives come from within, from the joy of young people. Christianity is perhaps acquiring another face and, also, another cultural form. It does not hold the command post in world opinion; others rule there. But it is the vital force without which even the other things would not continue. In this regard, thanks to what I myself am able to see and experience, I am quite optimistic that Christianity is on the verge of a new dynamic.

Do we nevertheless get the impression sometimes that by some law of nature paganism again and again wins back to some extent areas that were cleared and cultivated by Christianity?

In keeping with man's fallen nature, paganism breaks through in him again and again: this is an experience that runs through all the centuries. The truth of original sin is confirmed. Again and again man falls behind the faith and wants to be just himself again; he becomes a heathen in the most profound sense of the word. But again and again the divine presence in man becomes evident also. This is the struggle that passes through all of history. As Saint Augustine said: World history is a battle between two forms of love. Love of self—to the point of destroying the world. And love of others—to the point of renouncing oneself. This battle, which could always be seen, is in progress now, too.

6. Time for Conversion

At the beginning of the third millennium the peoples of the earth are experiencing an upheaval of hitherto unimaginable proportions, economically, ecologically, socially. Scientists regard the next decade as decisive for the continued existence of the planet.

Holy Father, you yourself in January 2009 used dramatic words in addressing diplomats in Rome: "Our future is at stake, as well as the fate of our planet." Unless we manage soon to introduce conversion on a broader basis, you said in another passage, the helplessness and the scenario of chaos would be intensified enormously. In Fatima your homily had an almost apocalyptic tone: "Mankind has succeeded in unleashing a cycle of death and terror, but failed in bringing it to an end. . . ." Do you see in the signs of the time signals of a world-altering caesura?

There are of course signs that frighten us, that worry us. But there are also other signs with which we can connect and which give us hope. We have indeed spoken at length already about the scenario of terror and danger. I would add here one more thing from the visits by the bishops that burns inside of me.

Many, many bishops, above all from Latin America, tell me that wherever the road of drug production and trafficking passes—and that includes large sectors of these countries—it is as if an evil monster had its hand on the country and had corrupted the people. I believe we do not always have an adequate idea of the power of this serpent of drug trafficking and consumption that spans the globe. It destroys youth, it destroys families, it leads to violence and endangers the future of entire nations.

This, too, is one of the terrible responsibilities of the West: that it uses drugs and that it thereby creates countries that have to supply it, which in the end exhausts and destroys them. A craving for happiness has developed that cannot content itself with things as they are. And that then flees into the devil's paradise, if you will, and destroys people all around.

And then there is a further problem. The destruction that sex tourism wreaks on our young people, the bishops say, is something we cannot even begin to imagine. The destructive processes at work in that are extraordinary and are born from the arrogance and the boredom and the false freedom of the Western world.

You see, man strives for eternal joy; he would like pleasure in the extreme, would like what is eternal. But when there is no God, it is not granted to him and it cannot be. Then he himself must now create something that is fictitious, a false eternity.

This is a sign of the times that should be an urgent challenge to us, especially as Christians. We have to show— and also live this accordingly—that the eternity man needs can come only from God. That God is the first thing necessary in order to be able to withstand the afflictions of this time. That we must mobilize, so to speak, all the powers of the soul and of the good so that a genuine coin can stand up against the false coin—and in this way the cycle of evil can be broken and stopped.

Looking at the end of natural resources, the end of an old epoch, the end of a particular way of life, we become aware again in a fundamental way of the finiteness of things—and also of the end of life in general. Many people see already in the signs of this time the portent of an end time. Maybe the world is not going under, they say, but it is going in a new direction. A society that has become sick, in which psychological problems especially are on the increase, longs for healing and redemption and is actually begging for it.

Shouldn't we reflect also on whether this new direction might possibly be connected with Christ's Second Coming?

The important thing, as you say, is that a need for healing exists, that man can understand again somehow what redemption means. Man recognizes that if God is not there, existence becomes sick and man cannot survive like that. That he needs an answer that he himself cannot give. In that respect this time is a time of Advent that also offers much that is good. The great communication, for example, that we have today can lead, on the one hand, to complete depersonalization. Then one is just swimming in a sea of communication and no longer encounters persons at all. But, on the other hand, it can also be an opportunity. For instance, to become aware of one another, to encounter one another, to help each other, to go out of ourselves.

So it seems to me important not to see only the negative side. While we must be very keenly aware of it, we must also see all the opportunities for good that are there; the hopes, the new possibilities for being human that exist. So as then, finally, to proclaim the need for change, which cannot happen without an interior conversion.

What does that mean concretely?

Part of this conversion is putting God in first place again. That changes everything else. And inquiring about God's words, so as to allow them as realities to shine into one's own life. We must, so to speak, dare again the experiment with God—so as to allow him to work within our society.

The Gospel, according to its own understanding, does not contain a message from the past that is over and done with. The presence and dynamism of Christ's revelation consists, on the contrary, precisely in the fact that it comes, in a way, from the future—and in turn is of decisive importance for the future of each individual as well as for the future of all. Christ, it says in the Letter to the Hebrews, "will appear a second time, not to deal with sin but to save those who are eagerly waiting for him".

Shouldn't the Church today explain much more clearly that, according to the statements in the Bible, the world finds itself no longer merely in the time after Christ, but rather again in the time before Christ?

Indeed, it was a concern of John Paul II to make clear that we are looking ahead to the coming of Christ. That consequently the One who has come is also, even more so, the One who is to come and that, from this perspective, we should live out our faith toward the future. Part of this is being really in a position to present the message of faith again from the perspective of the coming Christ.

Often this One who is coming has been presented in formulas that, while true, are nevertheless at the same time outmoded. They no longer speak to our living situation and are often no longer comprehensible to us. Or else this One who is coming is completely emptied and falsified, turned into a meaningless universal moral commonplace, so that nothing comes of it. We must therefore try in fact to express the substance as such—but to say it in a new way. Jürgen Habermas[1] has remarked that it is important that there be theologians who are able to translate the treasure that is preserved in their faith in such a way that in the secular world it is a word for this world. His understanding of this may be somewhat different from ours, but he is right that the intrinsic translation process of the great words into the speech and thinking of our time is under way but has really not yet succeeded. It can be successful only if people live Christianity in terms of the One who is coming. Only then can they also declare it. The declaration, the intellectual translation, presupposes the existential translation. In this respect the saints are the ones who live out their Christianity in the present and in the future, and the Christ who is coming can also be translated in terms of their existence, so that he can become present within the horizon of the secular world's understanding. That is the great task we face.

The changes of our time have brought other life-styles and philosophies of life with them, but also a different perception of the Church. Advances in medical research pose enormous ethical challenges. The new universe of the Internet, too, demands answers. John XXIII seized upon the change after the two world wars so as to interpret the "signs of the time", as he put it in the bull of convocation Humanae salutis, *dated December 25, 1961, as*

---

[1] Jürgen Habermas, a German philosopher and sociologist, born on June 18, 1929.

pointing to a council, even though he was already at that time an old, sick man.

Will Benedict XVI do the same?

Well, now, John XXIII made a great, unrepeatable gesture in entrusting to a general council the task of understanding the word of faith today in a new way. Above all, the Council took up and carried out its great mission of defining in a new way the Church's purpose as well as her relation to the modern era, and also the relation of faith to this time with its values. But to put into practice what was said, while remaining within the intrinsic continuity of the faith, is a much more difficult process than the Council itself. Especially since the Council came into the world in the interpretation devised by the media more than with its own documents, which are hardly ever read by anyone.

I think that our major task now, after a few fundamental questions are clarified, is first of all to bring to light God's priority again. The important thing today is to see that God exists, that God matters to us, and that he answers us. And, conversely, that if he is omitted, everything else might be as clever as can be—yet man then loses his dignity and his authentic humanity and, thus, the essential thing breaks down. That is why, I think, as a new emphasis we have to give priority to the question about God.

Do you think that the Catholic Church could really get around having the Third Vatican Council?

In all we have had more than twenty councils, and surely there will be another one someday. At the moment I do not see the prerequisites for it. I believe that at the moment the bishops' synods are the right instrument, in which the entire episcopate is represented and is, so to speak, "searching", keeping the whole Church together and at the same time leading her forward. Whether then some-day the moment will come again to do this in a major council, that we should leave to the future. At the moment we need, above all, those spiritual movements in which the universal Church, drawing upon her current experi-ences and at the same time coming from the interior experience of faith and of its power, sets up guideposts—and thereby makes God's presence the central focus again.

As the successor of Peter you recall again and again the decisive "plan" that exists for this world. Not a Plan A or some Plan B, but rather God's plan. "God is not indifferent to human events", you proclaimed; ultimately Christ is "the Lord of all creation and of all history". Karol Wojtyła had the task of lead-ing the Catholic Church over the threshold of the third millen-nium. What task does Joseph Ratzinger have?

I would say that one should not fragment history too much. We are weaving one and the same cloth. Karol Wojtyła was sent by God to the Church, so to speak, in a very specific, critical situation, in which, on the one hand, the Marxist generation, the 1968 generation, called the entire West into question and in which, conversely, real Socialism fell to pieces. In the midst of this conflict to open a path for a breakthrough to faith and to show that it is the center and the way—that was a historic moment of a special sort. Not every pontificate has to have a brand new task. Now it is a matter of continuing this and grasping the drama of the time, holding fast in that drama to the Word of God as the decisive word—and at the same time giving Christianity that simplicity and depth without which it cannot be effective.

PART II

THE PONTIFICATE

7. Habemus Papam

Rarely before in a papal election has the vote been so fast and so unanimous. Even after the first ballots in the Sistine Chapel, the results "moved dynamically toward the new Pope", as Curia Cardinal Walter Kasper reports. You yourself uttered in the conclave a fervent prayer like the one we know from the Garden of Gethsemane: "Lord, don't do this to me! You have younger and better men."

Seeing the unbelievable now actually happen was really a shock. I was convinced that there were better and younger candidates. Why the Lord settled on me, I had to leave to him. I tried to keep my equanimity, all the while trusting that he would certainly lead me now. I would have to grow slowly into what I could do in each given situation and always limit myself to the next step.

I find in particular this saying of the Lord so important for my whole life: "Do not be anxious about tomorrow.... Let the day's own trouble be sufficient for the day." One trouble a day is enough for man; more he cannot bear. That is why I try to concentrate on clearing away today's trouble and to leave the rest for tomorrow.

On the balcony of Saint Peter's Basilica, you said with a trembling voice during your first appearance that "after the great Pope

John Paul II" God had now chosen "a simple and humble laborer in the vineyard of the Lord". It comforted you to think that the Lord "knows how to work ... even with inadequate instruments". Now was that a papal understatement? After all, there were good reasons for electing you. No one has so publicly and intensively tackled the major issues as you have as a theologian: the relativism of modern society, the intra-ecclesial debate about the structure of the Church, reason and faith in the age of modern science. As Prefect of the Congregation for the Doctrine of the Faith, you helped shape the preceding pontificate. The Catechism of the Catholic Church, *one of the mammoth undertakings of the Wojtyła era, was produced under your direction.*

I did have a supervisory role, but I did nothing alone but was able to work in a team. Precisely as someone, among many others, who collaborates in the harvest of the Lord's vineyard. As foreman, perhaps, but nevertheless as someone who is not qualified to be the first and to carry the responsibility for the whole. So there was nothing left for me but to admit that there must be, besides the great Popes, little ones also, who give what they can. In this sense I said what I really felt at that moment.

For twenty-four years you stood at the side of John Paul II and knew the Curia like no one else. How long was it, though, until you fully realized how enormous the scope of this office really is?

One realizes very quickly that it is an immense office. If one knows that one already has a great responsibility as a chaplain, as a pastor, as a professor, then it is easy to extrapolate what an immense burden is imposed on the one who bears responsibility for the whole Church. But then of course one must be all the more aware that one does not do it alone. That one does it, on the one hand, with

God's help and, on the other hand, in a great collaboration. Vatican II correctly taught us that collegiality is a constitutive element in the structure of the Church. That the Pope can only be first together with others and not someone who would make decisions in isolation as an absolute monarch and do everything himself.

Saint Bernard of Clairvaux in the twelfth century, at the request of Pope Eugene III, composed an examination of conscience with the title "What a Pope Must Consider". Bernard had a sincere dislike for the Roman Curia and recommended to the Pope vigilance above all else. In the commotion of business he must find detachment, maintain oversight, and continue to be decisive with regard to the abuses that a Pope in particular finds on every side. He feared most of all, Bernard writes, "that you, surrounded by business matters, the number of which only increases until you see no end to them, might harden your heart".

Can you understand these "considerations" now from your own experience?

The "Consideration" by Saint Bernard is of course required reading for every Pope. There are great things in it, too, for example: Remember that you are not the successor of Emperor Constantine but rather the successor of a fisherman.

The basic theme is the one that you have noted: Do not become utterly absorbed in activism! There would be so much to do that one could be working on it constantly. And that is precisely the wrong thing. Not becoming totally absorbed in activism means maintaining *consideratio*, discretion, deeper examination, contemplation, time for interior pondering, vision, and dealing with things, remaining with God and meditating about God. One should not feel obliged to work ceaselessly; this in itself is important for everyone, too, for instance, for every manager, too, and even more so for a Pope. He has to leave many things to others so as to maintain his inner view of the whole, his interior recollection, from which the view of what is essential can proceed.

Nevertheless, people have the impression that Pope Benedict is constantly busy, that he never takes a break.

No; well....

You are one of the most diligent, perhaps even the most diligent worker of all the Popes.

But part of that is always meditation, reading Sacred Scripture, reflecting on what it says to me. One cannot simply work only on files. I do read as much there as I can. But I keep in mind the exhortation of Saint Bernard that one must not lose oneself in activism.

Paul VI, on the evening of his election as Pope, wrote in his diary: "I find myself in the papal chambers. A profound sense of uneasiness and confidence at the same time.... Then it is night, prayer and silence; no, it is not silence: the world watches and overtakes me. I must learn really to love it, the Church as she is, the world as it is."

Did you too, like Paul VI at the beginning, have a little fear of the masses of humanity whom you now must confront? Paul VI had even considered discontinuing the Angelus prayer at the window of the Apostolic Palace. He wrote, "What is this need to see a person? We have become a spectacle."

Yes, I understand the feelings of Paul VI very well. Here is the question: Is it really right for someone to present himself again and again to the crowd in that way and allow oneself to be regarded as a star? On the other hand, people have an intense longing to see the Pope. It is not so much a question then of contact with the person as it is of being physically in touch with this office, with the representative of the Holy One, with the mystery that there is a successor to Peter and someone who must stand for Christ. In this sense, then, one has to accept it and not refer the jubilation to oneself as a personal compliment.

Are you afraid of an assassination attempt?

No.

The Catholic Church is the first and greatest global player in world history. But everyone knows that she is not a business enterprise and the Pope is not a chief executive. How is it different from leading a multinational business empire?

Well, we are not a production plant, we are not a for-profit business, we are Church. That means a community of men standing together in faith. The task is not to manufacture some product or to be a success at selling merchandise. Instead, the task is to live the faith in an exemplary way, to proclaim it and at the same time to keep this voluntary association, which cuts across all cultures, nations, and times and is not based on external interests, spiritually connected with Christ and so with God himself.

Were there mistakes at the beginning?

Probably. But I cannot tell now what in particular. Maybe one makes even more mistakes later, because one is no longer so careful.

Was the feeling of being locked up, though, a little oppressive at first? In other words, does the Pope sometimes, to put it casually, get away once in a while on the sly?

I don't do that. But the fact that one can no longer simply go on an excursion, visit friends, or just be at home, that I cannot simply be in my house in Pentling again like I used to, walk together with my brother into the city, and go into a restaurant or look at something by myself is of course a loss. But the older you get, the less one takes the initiative, and in this respect one also puts up more easily with that loss.

Some think that the Pope is in a sort of isolation. That he breathes only filtered air and does not get any real sense of what is going on "out there". That he is not at all acquainted with the cares and needs of people.

Of course I cannot read all the newspapers and meet with an unlimited number of people. But there are, I believe, few people who have as many meetings as I do. Most important of all to me are my meetings with the bishops from all over the world. These are men who have both feet on the ground, and they do not come here because they would like something; they come in order to speak with me about the Church in their locality and about life in their locality. So in this way I can, after all, encounter the things of this world very humanly, personally, and realistically and observe them from an even closer perspective than from the newspaper. In this way I get a lot of background information.

Once in a while a mother comes along or a sister or a friend and would like to tell me one thing or another. There are, then, not just official visits but visits with quite a lot of human features. Then of course I find the papal household invaluable. In addition, friends from old times come to visit. All in all, therefore, I cannot say that I live in an artificial world of courtly personages; on the contrary, through these many meetings I experience very directly and personally the normal, everyday world of this time.

Does the Pope follow the news each day?

That too, of course.

History has already seen instances of Pope and anti-Pope. But seldom—or perhaps never before—have there been two successors of Peter whose pontificates were fused together—into a sort of millennial pontificate, so to speak—as John Paul II and Benedict XVI. Your predecessor was concerned with social problems worldwide, especially in Eastern Europe, whereas today the emphasis is more on the Church herself. Could one say that because of the ways in which John Paul II and Benedict XVI are different, they complement one another perfectly? The one, so to speak, plowed—the other sows. The one opened—the other fills?

That might be saying too much. Time does go on, too. Meanwhile another new generation is here with new problems. The 1968 generation with its peculiarities is established and past. The next generation, which then was more pragmatic, is aging already, too. Today the question is in fact: How do we manage in a world that is threatening itself, in which progress becomes a danger? Shouldn't we make a fresh start with God?

The question about God confronts the new generation again, but in a different way. And the new generation in the Church is different, too; it is more positive than the breakthrough generation of the 1970s.

You have stepped up to devote yourself to an inner renewal of the Church. As you put it, it is necessary "to ensure that [God's] Word continues to be present in its greatness and to resound in its purity, so that it is not torn to pieces by continuous changes in usage". In your book about Jesus we read: "The Church and the individual need constant purification.... What has become too big must be brought back to the simplicity and poverty of the Lord himself." In the business world one would say: Back to the beginning, to our core competence. What specifically does this inner renewal mean for your pontificate?

It means finding out where what is superficial and unnecessary is being dragged along—and, on the other hand, learning how we can succeed better at doing what is essential, so that we can really hear God's Word, live it out, and proclaim it in this time.

The Year of Saint Paul and the Year for Priests were two attempts at initiatives along these lines. To draw attention to the figure of Paul is to set the gospel before us in its original vitality, simplicity, and radicality, to make it present again. Precisely at a time when the sacrament of Holy Orders had been defiled so much, the Year for Priests was also supposed to present again in its beauty the unchangeable, unique task of this office, despite all the sufferings, despite all the horrible things. We must try to combine the humility and the greatness, so as to encourage priests again and give them joy in the priesthood.

The synods, too, help with this approach, for example, the Synod on the Word of God. Even the exchanges on this subject were very important. Today it is a question of setting forth the major themes and at the same time—as with the *caritas* encyclical, *God Is Love*—making visible again the center of Christian life and thus the simplicity of being a Christian.

One of your major themes is building a bridge between religion and rationality. Why do faith and reason belong together? Couldn't we also simply "just" believe? Jesus says, "Blessed are they who do not see and yet believe."

Not seeing is one thing, but even the faith of someone who does not see has to have its reasons. Jesus himself made faith thoroughly understandable by presenting it with an inner unity and in continuity with the Old Testament, with all of God's commands: as faith in the God who is the Creator and the Lord of history, to whom history testifies and about whom creation speaks.

It is interesting that this essential rationality is already in the Old Testament a fundamental component of the faith; that particularly in the time of the Babylonian exile it is said: "Our God is not one or another of many; he is the Creator; the God of heaven; the one God." Thereby a claim is made, the universality of which was based precisely on its reasonableness. This core concept later became the meeting place between the Old Testament and Greek civilization. For at approximately the same time as the Babylonian exile singled out in particular this feature of the Old Testament, Greek philosophy also developed, which now looked beyond the gods and inquired about the one God.

Today it is still the major task of the Church to unite faith and reason with each other, to write looking beyond what is tangible and rational responsibility at the same time. For after all, reason was given to us by God. It is what distinguishes man.

Now what is the special charism that a Pope brings with him from Germany? The Germans for almost a thousand years were responsible for the Holy Roman Empire. Delving deeply for knowledge is one of the fundamental themes in German cultural history, as exemplified by mystics like Meister Eckhart, polymaths like Albertus Magnus, and on down to Goethe, Kant, and Hegel. Germany, admittedly, is also the land of schism, the cradle of scientific communism, which promised paradise, not in heaven, but on earth. And last but not least it is the scene of a truly diabolical regime that called for the total destruction of the Jews, the Chosen People of God.

As you have indicated, in Germany we have a complex, contradictory, and dramatic history. A history full of guilt and full of suffering. But also a history with human greatness. A history of holiness. A history of great intellectual achievement. In that respect there is not simply one German charism.

You pointed out that another particular feature of a German cultural history is thoughtfulness. For a long time this trait was viewed as characteristic. Today people would probably view talents such as enterprise, energy, or efficiency as typically German instead. I think that God, if he was going to make a professor Pope in the first place, wanted this element of thoughtfulness and precisely this struggle for the unity of faith and reason to come to the fore.

8. In the Shoes of the Fisherman

The dark circles under your eyes, if I may say so, became the hallmark of your newly begun pontificate. At the end of the John Paul II era, it is said, there was still quite a lot of unfinished business, which had been left unattended on account of his illness.

Certainly John Paul II sometimes put off making decisions. But on the whole, business was very much attended to, thanks to the collaborators whom he had chosen. And he continued to make the major decisions, as he had always done. He was suffering, but he was also fully aware. The apparatus of the Church, if you will, was quite definitely in action.

It is no secret that John Paul II did not take any particularly energetic part or interest in the affairs of the Roman Curia.

Nevertheless, he did undertake the reform of the Curia, and he did give it its present structure. Even though he subsequently left many decisions to his collaborators, he always kept the whole in view, and he very definitely exercised the main responsibilities himself.

Is it possible that his long illness also stalled plans for reform that would otherwise have been initiated much sooner?

I don't think so. He had set such major priorities that, after all the big initiatives, the many new proclamations, the encyclicals, and the trips, each with its own agenda, it was actually almost a necessity for us to take the time needed to ponder and assimilate these things. And he produced moving new texts even in the latest part of his pontificate. One example is the apostolic letter *Tertio Millennio Adveniente*, which was written in preparation for the millennial year 2000. The text is suffused with warmth, almost with poetry.

The time of his suffering was no empty one, then. I think it was very important for the Church herself to receive this lesson in suffering after a great burst of activity and to see that the Church can also be governed through suffering and that it is precisely through suffering that she grows to maturity and is enlivened.

It looked as though this suffering might actually turn the capsized barque of Peter right side up again. Almost overnight, there emerged a generation of devout young people that had almost completely escaped notice until then.

There was a massive sense of solidarity with his suffering. You could see that the lesson of the suffering Pope was a magisterium that was even more eloquent than the magisterium of the speaking Pope. The sense of compassion, of profound emotion, the encounter in a certain sense with the suffering Christ touched people's hearts more deeply than the achievements of his active phase. The result was really a new beginning, also a new love for this Pope. I wouldn't say that this produced a complete about-face in the Church. After all, there are so many actors, and so many actions, at work on the stage of world history. But it was a sign in which the power of the Cross was suddenly revealed.

Jewish organizations welcomed your election as the 265th leader of the universal Church with an enthusiasm second to none. Israel Singer, at the time President of the World Jewish Congress, stated that, already during his tenure as Prefect of the Congregation for the Doctrine of the Faith, Joseph Ratzinger had articulated the underpinnings for the rapprochement between the two world religions. Singer went on to add that you had "changed the two-thousand year history of relations between Judaism and Christianity" for the better.

You were the first Pope to invite a rabbi to address a synod of bishops. You halted the beatification process of a French priest who was alleged to have made anti-Semitic speeches. You have visited more synagogues than all of your predecessors in the papal office. At the time of your election, the German newspaper Süddeutsche Zeitung *reported that "in his writings he professes the Jewish origins of Christianity more eloquently than any Pope before him."*

Your very first official act as Successor of Peter was a letter to the Jewish community of Rome. Was this symbolic gesture meant to convey a basic thrust of the pontificate?

Absolutely. I must say that from the very first day when I began to study theology, the intrinsic unity of the Old and the New Covenants, of the two parts of Holy Scripture, was somehow immediately clear to me. I realized that we can read the New Testament only together with what preceded it; otherwise, we would completely fail to understand it. Then as Germans we were of course shaken by what had happened in the Third Reich, which gave us a special reason to look with humility and shame, and with love, upon the People of Israel. As I have just said, it was already during my theological studies that these things came together and began to shape the course of my thinking as a theologian. For this reason it was clear to me—here, too, in full continuity with Pope John Paul II—that this new, loving, sympathetic interrelation of Israel and the Church, where each respects the being and distinctive mission of the other, had to play an essential part in my proclamation of the Christian faith.

Your predecessor called the Jews "our elder brothers". You speak of them as our "fathers in the faith".

The phrase "elder brothers", which had already been used by John XXIII, is not so welcome to Jews. The reason is that, in the Jewish tradition, the "elder brother"—Esau—is also the brother who gets rejected. One can still use it, because it expresses an important point. But it is true that they are also our "fathers in the faith". And this way of putting it illustrates perhaps even more clearly the character of our relationship to each other.

After your installation in office, it quickly became clear that there was a new style in the Vatican. "His Hurriness", who would jet from event to event, was gone. There would be no more flood of audiences, whose number was now cut in half. You abolished the custom of kissing the Pope's hand—though no one followed the new protocol. Next the tiara, symbolizing the worldly side of papal power, disappeared from the Pope's coat of arms. There was still another change: your predecessor had adopted the custom of speaking in the first person. Benedict reintroduced the papal "we" after John Paul's "I". What was the reason for this change?

I would like to address just two points. Paul VI had already renounced the tiara ...

... and sold it to give money to the poor.

But it was still in the papal coat of arms, and now it has been removed from that, too. I did not simply get rid of the "I". Rather, I use both the "I" and the "we". For on many, many matters I am not simply expressing ideas that have happened to occur to Joseph Ratzinger, but I am speaking out of the common life of the Church's communion. In these cases, I am speaking, as it were, in intrinsic fellowship with my fellow believers—and I am expressing what we are in common and what we can believe in common. In this sense, the "we" has its legitimate role, not as a plural of majesty, but as a real expression of the fact of coming from others, of speaking through and with others. But where one says something personal in the role of "I", then the first person singular has its role to play as well. So both are used: the "I" and the "we".

You shortened your first synod of bishops, held in October 2005, from four to three weeks. In addition, you introduced free discussion and invited a larger number of "fraternal delegates" from other churches. At the same time, you reintroduced regular meetings with the heads of the dicasteries in order to foster mutual exchange in the Curia. Decisions regarding personnel, however, especially appointments to the circle of your closest collaborators, are occasionally seen as posing problems for you. Is this your weak point?

The shortening of the synod reflected, I think, the wishes of everyone involved. Four weeks is simply too long for a bishop to be away from his diocese, you see. Precisely one of the ways in which a bishop takes part in the governance of the universal Church is by *properly* governing his local church and assuring her inner cohesion. Experience has shown that the schedule can be tightened without any difficulties. It was indeed important for me that the participants not simply read prepared speeches without generating any dialogue, but that they would have the opportunity to speak freely from the heart and then to enter into genuine dialogue as well.

Personnel decisions are difficult, because no one can look into another person's heart and no one can be certain of not being deceived. For this reason, I am more cautious, more anxious in this area, and it is only after having consulted with a variety of people that I make these kinds of decisions. And I think that, in spite of everything, in the last few years there has been success in making a whole series of really good personnel decisions; even in the German episcopacy.

Observers have noted that members of religious orders have increasingly been assuming positions of responsibility in the Roman Curia. The Italian daily Il Foglio *has even spoken already of a "Copernican revolution" in the Vatican's personnel policy. Conversely, critics are only too ready to find evidence here of an "infiltration by fundamentalists". Is the appointment of priests belonging to religious orders, who are bound by vows of poverty, chastity, and obedience, a sort of antidote to careerism and love of intrigue, which are not unknown even in the Vatican?*

A series of religious have been appointed because the religious orders contain a pool of really good people who have great talents and are men of God. But it is not true that the percentage of religious has increased disproportionately. I try to find the right man for the job, whether he is a religious or a diocesan priest. The decisive thing is whether he has the right qualities, whether he is a man of God, a true man of faith, and, above all, a man of courage.

I think that courage is one of the chief qualities that a bishop and a Curia head have to have nowadays. One aspect of this courage is the refusal to bow to the dictate of opinions but, rather, to act on the basis of what one inwardly knows is right, even when it causes annoyance. And of course the candidates have to be people who have qualities of intellect, professionalism, and humanity, so that they can also lead and draw others into a close-knit community. For example, it was very important for me as the head of the Congregation for the Doctrine of the Faith for us to be a community, not to fight among or alongside one other, but to be a family. I set great store by this capacity to foster relationships and to enable teamwork.

A Pope always also speaks in gestures and actions, signs and symbols. It caused a stir when you chose the now famous camauro, a sort of peaked cap that had last been worn by John XXIII, as a head covering for the winter. Was that just a fashion accessory—or was it the expression of a return to tried and true forms in the Church?

I wore it only once. I was just cold, and I happen to have a sensitive head. And I said, since the camauro is there, then let's put it on. But I was really just trying to fight off the cold. I haven't put it on again since. In order to forestall over-interpretation.

9. Ecumenism and the Dialogue with Islam

Ecumenism quickly became the most conspicuous trademark of the present pontificate. The Pope pledged his commitment to work for "the restoration of full, visible unity" among Christians. Observers have seen it as a strategic coup that you devote so much attention to Orthodoxy, working to open the way to reunion where there is the most common ground.

Ecumenism is a multilayered, multifaceted phenomenon. It involves the whole of global Orthodoxy, which is already quite varied in itself, but also global Protestantism, whose classical confessions are quite different from the New Protestantism, the growth of which is one of the signs of the times. The place where we are, if you will, closest to home, and where there is also the most hope of reunion, is Orthodoxy.

Paul VI and John Paul II already devoted a great deal of effort to dialogue with Orthodoxy. I myself have always had very close contacts with Orthodoxy. When I was a professor in Bonn and Regensburg, I always had Orthodox among my students, and this gave me the opportunity to form many friendships in the Orthodox world. Catholics and Orthodox both have the same basic structure inherited from the ancient Church, and in that sense it was natural for me to take special pains to foster their encounter. I am very grateful for the cordiality shown me by Patriarch Bartholomew, who practices ecumenism as much more than a cold duty; there is a real friendship and sense of brotherhood between us. And I am also very grateful for the friendship and the great cordiality that Patriarch Kirill has shown me.

The Patriarch of Moscow, in fact, was the first visitor whom you received after your election as Pope.

At the time, he was not yet the Patriarch of the Russian Orthodox Church in Moscow but, rather, its foreign minister. We immediately got along. He has such a joy about him, such a simple faith—the simplicity of the Russian soul, you might say—but also its determination and warmth. So we understood each other well.

I do think it is very important for the great Orthodox world, with its internal tensions, also to see its interior unity with the worldwide Latin Church, with her very different style. Despite all the differences that have built up over the centuries on account of cultural separations and other factors, it is important that we truly relearn to see and understand our inner spiritual kinship with each other. On this level, I think we are making progress. I do not mean tactical, political progress, but rapprochement on the level of our interior affinity. I find this very consoling.

But why should this rapprochement have great significance for "the future history of the world", as you once stated?

Because it makes our common responsibility for the world plain for people to see again. It would, of course, be perfectly possible to keep arguing about all sorts of things.

Or, basing ourselves on what we have in common, we could render a common service instead. And, as our conversation has made clear, the world needs a well-founded, spiritually based, rationally bolstered capacity for witness to the one God who speaks to us in Christ. In this sense, our cooperation is enormously important. Kirill emphasizes the same thing as well, precisely in the debate concerning the major ethical issues. We are not moralistic, but, standing on the foundation of the faith, we are bearers of an ethical message that provides a compass for mankind. And it is of the greatest importance that we provide it together at this time when the peoples of the earth are in crisis.

According to Gerhard Ludwig Müller, a bishop known for his ecumenical engagement, Catholics and Orthodox have already achieved 97 percent of ecclesial unity. The remaining 3 percent consists, Müller says, in the question of papal primacy and jurisdiction. Not only did you remove the tiara as a symbol of authority from the papal coat of arms, but you also ordered the designation "Patriarch of the West" struck from the list of papal titles. The Bishop of Rome is, you said, only the first among equals. Significantly, even while still a cardinal, you stated in the declaration Dominus Iesus, which was issued in 2000, that genuine particular churches exist, "although they lack full communion with the Catholic Church, insofar as they do not accept the Catholic teaching of primacy."

Will Pope Benedict XVI restructure the papacy in order to foster the unity of Christianity?

A few qualifications would of course be needed here now. "First among equals" is not exactly the formula that we believe as Catholics. The Pope is the first—and he also has specific functions and tasks. In this respect, not everyone is equal. "First among equals" would be immediately acceptable to Orthodoxy; it acknowledges that the Bishop of Rome is the *protos*, the first, as is laid down already by the Council of Nicaea. But the question is precisely whether the Pope has specific tasks or not. The citation from *Dominus Iesus* is also complex. But these are contentious issues, which I would have to say more about than I can right now ...

Does that mean that Ratzinger as Pope is contradicting his earlier self as Cardinal and custodian of the faith?

No, what I defended was the heritage of the Second Vatican Council and of the entire history of the Church. The passage means that the Eastern Churches are genuine particular churches, although they are not in communion with the Pope. In this sense, unity with the Pope is not constitutive for the particular church. Nevertheless, the lack of unity is also an intrinsic lack in the particular church. For the particular church is ordered to membership in a whole. In this respect, non-communion with the Pope is a defect in the living cell of the particular church, as it were. It remains a cell, it is legitimately called a church, but the cell is lacking something, namely, its connection with the organism as a whole.

I would also be less confident than Bishop Müller and would be shy of saying that only 3 percent is still missing. First of all, there are huge historical and cultural differences. Beyond the doctrinal issues, there are still many steps to be taken at the level of the heart. God still needs to do some work on us here. For the same reason, I would also be shy about making any predictions about when reunion will happen. The important thing is that we truly love each other, that we have an interior unity, that we draw as close together and collaborate as much as we can—while trying to work through the remaining areas of open questions. And it is important for us always to remember in all of this that we need God's help, that we are incapable of doing this alone.

And yet the Greek Orthodox Metropolitan Augoustinos thinks that we are already at the point where a papal primacy of honor could be recognized by all Christians. Even the Lutheran Bishop Johannes Friedrich has raised the possibility of a limited recognition of the papal office as an "ecumenically acceptable spokesman of the world's Christians". Are you pointing in the same direction when you say that the churches today should take their inspiration from the example of the first millennium?

We could also add to the list the Anglicans who have said they could accept a primacy of honor on the part of the Pope of Rome, who, among other things, would function as a spokesman of the Christian world. That is, of course, already a significant step. And it is also true de facto that when the Pope takes a position on major ethical issues, the world regards him as speaking with the voice of all Christians. For his part, the Pope himself makes an effort to speak in such matters for all Christians, as it were, rather than placing the specifically Catholic position in the foreground. That has its place in a different context.

In this respect, it is already the case that the Bishop of Rome can speak to a certain extent for all Christians, simply on account of the position he has acquired in history. This is also an important ecumenical factor, which gives an outward form to an inward unity that has never been completely lost among Christians. The Pope's importance mustn't be overestimated. There are still plenty of sharp differences. But the existence of the kind of representation I have described is a cause for gratitude.

You have already met with the Ecumenical Patriarch of Constantinople. As for the Russian Orthodox Church, the Chair-man of the Department of External Church Relations, Archbishop Hilarion, has said that "we are approaching the point in time when it will be possible to start preparations for a meeting between the Pope and the Patriarch of Moscow." Such a meeting would be an international sensation. Do you think it could take place while you are still Pope?

That depends on how much life the good Lord grants me, but I hope so. It was already a very lovely gesture on the Patriarch's part to ask Hilarion to arrange a concert in Rome to celebrate the fifth anniversary of my pontificate; Hilarion is a composer himself, and he performed one of his compositions. So there are many forms of contact between us. Nevertheless, Orthodox public opinion in Russia has to be prepared for a meeting of this kind. There is still a certain fear of the Catholic Church. We need to wait patiently, and we mustn't rush things. But the will is there on both sides, and the context in which it can come to fruition is also developing.

A meeting between Rome and Moscow in the not too distant future is within the realm of possibility?

I would say that, yes.

There has also been progress on the question of church unity in China. At present, almost all of the bishops nominated by State authorities in China have also been recognized by Rome. Both sides have described union between the State-approved and the unofficial Catholic communities as a natural goal. What is your opinion: Can this reunion—supposing, as you said, that the Lord grants you a long life—still come about in the Era of Benedict?

I hope so. Jesus' prayer that all who believe in him may be one (Jn 17) is bearing its fruit in China. The whole Church that dwells in China is called to live in a deep spiritual unity, which must also enable the maturation of a harmonious hierarchical unity in communion with the Bishop of Rome. Of course, new stumbling blocks keep cropping up. But we have already come a long way. And as you said yourself, the great majority of the bishops who in the past had been consecrated without an apostolic mandate from Rome have since acknowledged the primacy and thus entered into communion with Rome. Even though unexpected difficulties always occur, there is much hope that we can definitively overcome the separation. This is a goal that is particularly dear to me and that I bring before the Lord daily in prayer.

What led to this turn of events, which until just a short time ago no one would have thought possible?

A variety of factors have favored the positive development of the Catholic Church in China. I will mention just some of them. On the one hand, a fervent desire to be in union with the Pope has never been absent among the illegitimately consecrated bishops. This made it possible for practically all of them to embark on the path to communion, a process during which we patiently accompanied them and worked with them one-on-one. There was a basic Catholic sense among them that said one is only really a bishop precisely in this communion. On the other hand, the secretly consecrated bishops, who were not approved by the State, can now profit from the fact that, even for purely political reasons, it is no longer advantageous for the government to imprison Catholic bishops and deprive them of their freedom on account of their allegiance to Rome. This is a nonnegotiable precondition of, and at the same time a decisive help to, the reestablishment of full union between the two Catholic communities.

It is the ecumenical dialogue with the Protestants that seems to have run into difficulties. Among orthodox Protestants, it is not on the agenda anyway; the divisions have become too deep. But even according to some Roman Catholic bishops, sectors of the Protestant churches have surrendered much of their tradition under the pressure of modernity. Since the 1970s, the trend among many Protestants, these bishops say, has gone first in a socialist, then in an ecological, and finally in a feminist direction, with a new tendency toward gender mainstreaming. These bishops also charge that those involved in dialogue are really aiming to protestantize the Catholic Church, which is portrayed as antiquated, in order to be able to create an image of themselves as a progressive alternative.

In the interest of avoiding further frustrations, wouldn't it be more honest to say: Yes, let us be friends, let us work together in concerted Christian action, but a reunion is unfortunately not possible—except at the cost of sacrificing our own identity.

First of all, we need to consider the vast, multilayered character of global Protestantism. Lutheranism, after all, is just one part of the spectrum of the Protestant world. There are also the Reformed, the Methodists, and so forth.

In addition, there is also the major new phenomenon of the Evangelicals, who are expanding with an enormous dynamism and are in the process of changing the whole religious landscape in the countries of the Third World. So when we talk about dialogue with Protestantism, we need to keep in mind this multifaceted character, which also varies from country to country.

We must recognize the fact that Protestantism has taken steps that have led it farther away from us, rather than closer to us; women's ordination and the acceptance of homosexual partnerships are just two of many similar examples. There are also other ethical positions, other instances of conformism with the spirit of the present age, that make the dialogue more difficult. At the same time, of course, there are also people in the Protestant communities who are pressing very energetically for the authentic substance of the faith and who do not approve of this attitude on the part of their denominations as a whole.

What we should be saying is this: As Christians, we have to find a common basis; as Christians we must be capable of speaking with a common voice about the major questions and of bearing witness to Christ as the living God. We are not going to bring about full unity in the foreseeable future, but let us do what we can. Let us join as real Christians in performing some task, in bearing some witness, in this world.

Is it really true that the Pope does not regard Protestants as a Church, but, unlike the Eastern Church, only as an ecclesial community? This distinction strikes many as demeaning.

The word "ecclesial community" is a term employed by the Second Vatican Council. The Council applied a very simple rule in these matters: A Church in the proper sense, as we understand it, exists where the episcopal office, as the sacramental expression of apostolic succession, is present—which also implies the existence of the Eucharist as a sacrament that is dispensed by the bishop and by the priest. If this is not the case, then we are dealing with the emergence of another model, a new way of understanding what a church is, which at Vatican II we designated by the term "ecclesial community". The word was intended to indicate that such communities embody a different mode of being a church. As they themselves insist, it is precisely not the same mode in which the Churches of the great tradition of antiquity are Churches, but is based on a new understanding, according to which a church consists, not in the institution, but in the dynamism of the Word that gathers people into a congregation.

This term, then, is an attempt to capture what is distinctive about Protestant Christianity and to give it a positive expression. We can always keep trying to find better terms, but the basic distinction is legitimate, indeed, it is a fact even from a purely historical point of view.

Apart from that, it is worth stressing again that the ecclesial situation differs greatly from one Protestant community to another. They define themselves differently even among themselves, so that we cannot speak of *the* Protestant Church. The key point is that Protestantism has, as it were, shifted the accent of Christianity and that we are trying to understand this, to acknowledge one another as Christians, and to join in service as Christians.

And not even a Pope can offer an alternative definition of a Church?

No. He has no authority over that. The Second Vatican Council is binding on him.

In its ecumenical dialogue with ecclesial communities in the West, the Vatican concentrates on the Anglicans, the Lutheran World Federation, the World Alliance of Reformed Churches, and the World Methodist Council. The gates of Rome are already open to Anglicans who are willing to swim the Tiber. You have promulgated an apostolic constitution for this purpose, which for the first time provides their own canonical and organizational structure for local churches. Prior to the constitution, the idea of reunion was associated with the image of a return home to the Latin Church. Is this a precedent for other groups that might want to follow in the footsteps of the Anglicans?

At any rate, it is an attempt to respond to a specific challenge. The initiative did not come from us, but from Anglican bishops who entered into dialogue with the Congregation for the Doctrine of the Faith in order to explore possible forms of reunion. They said that they fully share the faith that is set forth in the *Catechism of the Catholic Church*, that this is exactly what they believe. And they asked us to examine to what extent they might be able to preserve their own tradition, their own inherited form of life, with all of the riches it contains.

Eventually, the process resulted in the offer of this framework. It remains to be seen how much use is made of it, how much fruit it will really bear, and what kinds of developments and variations might be involved in it.

But it is at any rate a sign, you might say, of the flexibility of the Catholic Church. We don't want to create new uniate churches, but we do want to offer ways for local church traditions, traditions that have evolved outside of the Roman Church, to be brought into communion with the Pope and thus into Catholic communion.

Your Regensburg Lecture, *delivered on September 12, 2006, triggered a massive controversy that affected the relations between the Church and the Muslims. At a certain point in your talk, you cited a passage from a scholarly edition of a dialogue about Islam and Christianity that took place between the Byzantine emperor and an educated Persian.*[1] *In some Islamic countries, Christian places of worship subsequently went up in flames, while in the West journalists penned fiercely critical editorials.*

The lecture has been classified as the first mistake of the pontificate. Was it?

I had conceived and delivered the lecture as a strictly academic address, without realizing that people don't read papal lectures as academic presentations, but as political statements. The political reading ignored the fine web of the argument, ripping the passage out of its context and turning it into a political statement, which it wasn't. The text dealt with an exchange in an ancient dialogue, which, incidentally, I think is still of great interest. Emperor Manuel, who is cited in this passage, was at that time already

---

[1] The lecture, delivered at the university where Joseph Ratzinger had formerly taught as a professor, dealt with the topic of "Faith, Reason, and the University: Memories and Reflections". The passage in which Benedict XVI cites the late medieval Byzantine Emperor Manuel II Paleologus can be found in the appendix.

a vassal of the Ottoman Empire, so he could not very well attack Muslims. What he could do, though, was pose vital questions in the context of an intellectual dialogue. Unfortunately, however, the nature of present-day political communication prevents understanding of subtleties of context like this.

Nevertheless, after all the awful things that happened, about which I can only feel sadness, these events ultimately turned out to have a positive impact. During my visit to Turkey, I was able to show that I respect Islam, that I acknowledge it as a great religious reality with which we must be in dialogue. And so this controversy led to the development of a truly vigorous dialogue.

It became evident that Islam needs to clarify two questions in regard to public dialogue, that is, the questions concerning its relation to violence and its relation to reason. It was an important first step that now there was within Islam itself a realization of the duty and the need to clarify these questions, which has since led to an internal reflection among Muslim scholars, a reflection that has in turn become a theme of dialogue with the Church.

The Islamic newspaper Zaman *spoke of the Pope's "message of peace"; at long last, the paper went on to say, interreligious dialogue has gotten off the ground. Even German newspapers such as* Die Zeit, *after an initial round of harsh criticism, were now paying their respects to the "wise man in the East" who "is proving to be the most important authority of the West in the Islamic world".*

At any rate, things have since developed in a positive direction. As you know, 138 Islamic scholars wrote a letter containing an explicit invitation to dialogue and an interpretation of Islam that immediately placed it in dialogue with Christianity. I have also had a very good conversation about this with the king of Saudi Arabia. Like other Islamic heads of State, or also the kings of the Gulf States for example, he wants to make common cause with Christians against the abuse of Islam by terrorists. We know that today we are on the same side of a common battle. There are two things we have in common: we both defend major religious values—faith in God and obedience to God—and we both need to situate ourselves correctly in modernity. The Council for Interreligious Dialogue is also dealing with these topics. At issue are questions such as: What is tolerance? How are truth and tolerance related? In this context, the question of whether tolerance includes the right to change religions also emerges. It is hard for the Islamic partners to accept this. Their argument is that once someone has come to the truth, he can no longer turn back.

At any rate, we have entered into an extensive and vigorous relation of dialogue that is bringing us closer and teaching us to understand one another better. Which also just may help us to find more positive ways of facing this difficult hour of history together.

It was not so long ago, though, when the Popes thought it their duty to save Europe from Islamization. Is the Vatican now following a completely different policy?

No. Historical situations change. To take just one example, there was a time when the Ottoman Empire threatened the borders of Europe, laid siege to Europe, and, finally, stood before the gates of Vienna. Or think of the

Battle of Lepanto in 1571. At that point there was really a question of whether the identity of Europe would be preserved or whether Europe would become a colony. In this situation, in which the problem was not only Islam, but the expansion of Ottoman power, Europe had to stand united in defense of its history, its culture, and its faith.

Today we are living in a completely different world, in which the battle lines are drawn differently. In this world, radical secularism stands on one side, and the question of God, in its various forms, stands on the other. Of course the respective identity of the various religions must continue to exist. We cannot dissolve ourselves into one another. On the other hand, we must try to understand one another.

In large parts of Sub-Saharan Africa, there has been a long tradition of tolerant and good coexistence between Islam and Christianity. When I receive the bishops from these countries, they tell me that it is simply a matter of ancient custom for them to celebrate one another's holidays. In other parts of the world, the relationship is still characterized by intolerance and aggression. In this respect, the historical situations are still very different even today. In any case, we must try to live the grandeur of our faith and to embody it in a vital way, while, on the other hand, trying to understand the heritage of others. The important thing is to discover what we have in common and, wherever possible, to perform a common service in this world.

At the same time, it is impossible to overlook the fact that in countries where Islam dominates State and society, human rights are trampled upon and Christians are brutally oppressed. For the Anglican bishop Michael Nazir-Ali, Islam is the greatest threat to the West since Communism, because it involves, in his view, an encompassing political and socio-economic ideology. The President of the Islamic Republic of Iran, Mahmud Ahmadine-jad, has declared that the countdown has begun for the destruction of Israel, which he says will soon be "erased from the map".

Doesn't this suggest that the idea of dialogue with Islam is also a bit naïve, or even dangerous?

Islam is lived in very different ways, depending on its various historical traditions and on its provenance and the current relationships of power. In Sub-Saharan Africa, as we said, there is a welcome tradition of coexistence, at least in many regions, where it is also possible to change religions and where children of an Islamic father can become Christians. In these areas there exists a rapprochement on the level of the fundamental understanding of freedom and truth, a rapprochement that does not dampen the intensity of faith.

But where Islam has a, let's say, monocultural dominance, where its traditions and its cultural and political identity are uncontested, it easily sees itself in the role of a counterweight to the Western world, as the defender, you might say, of religion against atheism and secularism. The sense for truth then can narrow down to the point of becoming intolerance, thus making a coexistence with Christians very difficult. The important thing here is to remain in close contact with all the currents within Islam that are open to, and capable of, dialogue, so as to give a change of mentality a chance to happen even where Islamism still couples a claim to truth with violence.

10. Proclaiming the Gospel

Your very first publication, which appeared when you were still a student, was the translation of a text by Thomas Aquinas. It bore the title "On Love". Your first publication as Pope, which appeared exactly sixty years later, was an encyclical on the same topic: Deus caritas est, *God is love. A Pope's first encyclical is always regarded as a sort of key to his pontificate, is it not?*

As for that little work from my student days, Alfred Läpple had suggested that I translate Saint Thomas Aquinas' *Disputed Question on Charity*, because Martin Grabmann, the great medievalist, had said that the *Quaestiones* were still untranslated, and someone needed to translate them. But the translation did not actually get published. It was probably not a very good translation, either, since I wasn't even twenty years old at the time.... So, though I actually came to this topic by chance, I was fascinated by it. Two themes have always accompanied me in my life, then: on the one hand, the theme of Christ, as the living, present God, the God who loves us and heals us through suffering, and, on the other hand, the theme of love, which for its part occupies a central place in Johannine theology—because I knew that love is the key to Christianity, that love is the angle from which it has to be approached. Which is why I also wrote the first encyclical from the point of view of this key.

The Catholic Church's teaching on sexual morality provokes violent contradiction, a topic we will take up again later. In Deus caritas est, *the Pope explains that the "humanity of faith" includes man's Yes to his own bodiliness, which is part of God's creation. Were you making a case for better sex?*

Of course bodiliness encompasses far more than that, so we cannot define it simply in terms of sexuality, but sexuality is an essential component of bodiliness. The important point is that man is embodied soul, that he has his identity as a body, so that he ought to approach the body in a positive light and to understand sexuality as a positive gift. He himself takes part in God's creative action by means of sexuality. Finding this positive approach and protecting this treasure that has been given to us are very important tasks. Admittedly, forms of rigorism have also repeatedly gained ground in Christianity, and the tendency toward negative appraisals of sexuality, a tendency that had developed in Gnosticism, also found its way into the Church. Just think of Jansenism, which warped and intimidated people. It is evident today that we need to find our way back to the genuinely Christian attitude that existed among the first Christians and in the great periods of Christian culture: the attitude of joy in, and affirmation of, the body, of sexuality—seen as a gift that always requires discipline and responsibility as well.

The same thing applies here that applies everywhere: Freedom and responsibility belong together. For only then does real joy also grow, is a real Yes possible. This underscores the importance of setting forth afresh, as something positive, as a great affirmation, the Christian image of man, whose rediscovery was spurred by the teaching of Vatican II.

As in Deus caritas est, *in your next encyclical,* Spe salvi,[1] *and in the social encyclical* Caritas in veritate,[2] *that exhorts to social responsibility in politics and economy, you repeatedly speak of what you call "Christian existence". Even the non-theologian senses that this phrase indicates a kind of life that has nothing to do with the banal existence of the prosperous bourgeois. Does this mean that Christianity, as the Pope understands it, is accordingly more of a challenging, radical force that questions prevailing conventions? Especially because it says things that many people are too frightened even to consider?*

I would not want to offer a judgment about what has been thought in the past. But there does need to be a new realization that being human is something great, a great challenge, to which the banality of just drifting along doesn't do justice. Any more than the attitude that comfort is the best way to live, that feeling healthy is the sum and substance of happiness. There needs to be a new sense that being human is subject to a higher set of standards, indeed, that it is precisely these demands that make a greater happiness possible in the first place. There needs to be a sense that being human is like a mountain-climbing expedition that includes some arduous slopes. But it is by them that we reach the summit and are able to experience for the first time how beautiful it is to be. Emphasizing this is of particular concern to me.

One of the most controversial pronouncements of your pontificate so far is the motu proprio Summorum Pontificum, *which was issued in July of* 2007. *Its purpose was to make access*

[1] *Saved in Hope,* November 2007.
[2] *Charity in Truth,* June 2009.

easier to the earlier Latin Mass, which until then could be celebrated only with the permission of the local bishop. In an accompanying letter you expressly stated that the new vernacular liturgy remains the ordinary form, whereas the Tridentine Mass is the extraordinary form. You also stated that the central issue for you was not the "often petty questions regarding this or that form", but "the cosmic character of the liturgy", as well as the broad continuity of the Christian liturgy with the heritage of the Old Testament. What did you mean by this?

This is a very big topic. The essential point is to avoid celebrating the liturgy as an occasion for the community to exhibit itself, under the pretext that it is important for everyone to involve himself, though in the end, then, only the "self" is really important. Rather, the decisive thing is that we enter into something that is much greater. That we can get out of ourselves, as it were, and into the wide open spaces. For the same reason, it is also very important that the liturgy itself not be tinkered with in some way.

Liturgy, in truth, is an event by means of which we let ourselves be introduced into the expansive faith and prayer of the Church. This is the reason why the early Christians prayed facing east, in the direction of the rising sun, the symbol of the returning Christ. In so doing, they wanted to show that the whole world is on its way toward Christ and that he encompasses the whole world. This connection between heaven and earth is very important. It was no accident that ancient churches were built so that the sun would cast its light into the house of God at a very precise moment. Nowadays we are rediscovering the importance of the interactions between the earth and the rest of the universe, and so it makes perfect sense that we should also relearn to recognize the cosmic character of the liturgy. As well as its historical character. Which means recognizing that someone didn't just one day invent the liturgy, but that it has been growing organically since the time of Abraham. These kinds of elements from the earliest times are still present in the liturgy.

Concretely, the renewed liturgy of the Second Vatican Council is the valid form in which the Church celebrates liturgy today. My main reason for making the previous form more available was to preserve the internal continuity of Church history. We cannot say: Before, everything was wrong, but now everything is right; for in a community in which prayer and the Eucharist are the most important things, what was earlier supremely sacred cannot be entirely wrong. The issue was internal reconciliation with our own past, the intrinsic continuity of faith and prayer in the Church.

On the other hand, the decision stirred up a controversy surrounding the petition for the conversion of the Jews that was contained in the Good Friday liturgy of the old Mass. The New York rabbi and historian Jacob Neusner defended this petition, arguing that it reflects "the logic of monotheism". Even believing Jews, Neusner pointed out, pray three times a day that eventually all non-Jews will call upon the name of YHWH.

You eventually had the text replaced by new wording in February 2008. Could you understand the arguments of the critics?

First of all, I am very grateful to Rabbi Neusner for what he said, because it was genuinely helpful. Second: this petition does not affect the liturgy in general, but only the small circle of people who use the old missal.[3] So

---

[3] The missal is the book used for Mass in the Roman Catholic rite.

there was no question of any change in the main liturgy. But in the old liturgy this point seemed to me to require a modification. The old formulation really was offensive to Jews and failed to express positively the overall intrinsic unity between the Old and New Testament. For this reason, I believed that a modification of this passage in the old liturgy was necessary, especially, as I have already said, out of consideration for our relation with our Jewish friends. I altered the text in such a way as to express our faith that Christ is the Savior for *all*, that there are not two channels of salvation, so that Christ is *also* the redeemer of the Jews, and not just of the Gentiles. But the new formulation also shifts the focus from a direct petition for the conversion of the Jews in a missionary sense to a plea that the Lord might bring about the hour of history when we may all be united. So the polemical arguments with which a whole series of theologians assailed me are ill-considered; they do not accurately reflect the reality of the situation.

Your motu proprio Omnium in mentem, *to which scant attention has been paid since its publication in December* 2009, *modifies canon law regarding the diaconate and marriage. Henceforth the validity of marriage is not affected by the fact that one of the parties, though a baptized Catholic, has left the Church, say, for tax purposes.*[4] *According to the motu proprio, the goal of the emendation is equal treatment for all Catholics. But isn't this*

---

[4] In Germany, the government collects for the major churches from church members. Someone who declares to government officials that he has left the church no longer has to pay this tax and is no longer considered a member of the church. Recently, there have been discussions about whether someone can still be considered a member of the church even though he is no longer a member under civil law.

tantamount to saying that someone can declare he is leaving the Church for official tax purposes—and yet remain a member of the Church?

You raise an issue I cannot resolve here. It concerns a truly major dispute that is going on between Germany and Rome right now: To what extent is membership in a public corporation that collects taxes for ecclesiastical purposes identical with membership in the Mystical Body of Christ that the Church incarnates? Obviously the Church also needs a concrete institutional structure. She also needs a bodily presence. She needs external juridical forms. And of course part of being Christian includes doing something for one's own community. The German system is completely unique, and it is currently the object of a very significant and, as I believe, also very salutary dispute between the organs of the Holy See and the German Bishops' Conference. I do not wish to anticipate its outcome.

There was surprise when you decided to approve the "heroic virtue" for Pius XII, a prerequisite for his beatification. At the same time, this decree did not involve any historical or political judgment, but only an assessment of his activity as a pastor.

The public image of Eugenio Pacelli, who reigned from 1939 to 1958 as Pius XII, has been largely shaped by the work of the dramatist Rolf Hochhuth, who portrays Pius as a ruthless power broker indifferent to the destiny of the Jews. As scholars have since shown, this figure has practically nothing in common with the actual Pius XII. According to historian Karl-Joseph Hummel, under Pius XII as many as 150,000 Jews were saved from the Nazi extermination camps with the help of the Catholic Church.

The Jewish philosopher Bernard-Henri Lévy stated that the 1937 encyclical Mit brennender sorge, *which Pacelli helped pen as Cardinal Secretary of State, is even today still one of the "most resolute and eloquent manifestos against the Nazis". As Pope, Pius XII saw to it that "the monasteries were opened to the persecuted Jews of Rome." In 1958, Golda Meir, later Prime Minister of Israel, stated that "when a horrific martyrdom was visited upon our people in the decade of the National Socialist terror, the Pope lifted up his voice on behalf of the victims."*

And yet some Jewish communities expressed considerable reservations. Should not the Church have waited until all the Vatican archives had been opened?

Actually, the recognition of heroic virtue, which, as you have already said, is not an assessment of his political and historical achievements as such, had already been worked on for two years. At first, I did not grant my signature, but I ordered an inspection of the unpublished archival records, because I wanted to be absolutely sure. Obviously it was impossible to evaluate the papers, of which there are hundreds of thousands, in a rigorously scientific manner. But it was possible to reconfirm our original impression of the whole and to see that the records confirm the positive things we know, but not the negative things that are alleged. You have already pointed out yourself that Pius XII saved thousands of Jewish lives, for example, by ordering the convents and cloisters of Rome to open their doors—something only the Pope himself can do—and declaring them extraterritorial, which was a not completely secure position legally, but which was nonetheless tolerated by the Germans after the fact. It is perfectly clear that as soon as he protested publicly, the Germans would have ceased to respect extraterritoriality, and the thousands who had found a safe haven in the monasteries of Rome would surely have been deported.

In this respect, it was simply a matter of many lives that could only have been saved this way. It just recently came to light that Pacelli, already as Secretary of State, had written to all the bishops of the world in 1938, instructing them to take pains to ensure that visas were generously granted to Jews emigrating from Germany. For his part, he did all that he could to save people. Of course one can still always ask "Why didn't he protest more clearly?" I believe it was because he saw what consequences would follow from an open protest. We know that personally he suffered greatly because of it. He knew he actually ought to speak out, and yet the situation made that impossible for him.

At the present time, we have new clever people who say that, while he did save many lives, he had old-fashioned ideas about the Jews that fall short of the teaching of Vatican II. But that is not the question. The decisive thing is what he did and what he tried to do, and on that score we really must acknowledge, I believe, that he was one of the great righteous men and that he saved more Jews than anyone else.

11. The Journeys of a Shepherd

The Pope may not be the most powerful man in the world, but his appearances can be events that reach millions of people around the globe, more than any pop star. Before becoming Pope you weren't exactly considered a tribune of the people. Do you get stage fright?

Of course I am sometimes concerned, and I wonder whether I can I make it even from a purely physical point of view. The trips are always very demanding for me. I actually don't get stage fright, though, since everything is well-prepared. So I know that now I am no longer speaking for myself, but that I am simply there for the Lord—and that I don't need to worry whether I look good, whether I am well-received, and that sort of thing. I am carrying out the task entrusted to me, in the awareness that this is being done for Another and that this Other is standing by me. This enables the trips to go ahead without a sense of fear on my part.

Your predecessor was certainly regarded as what you might call a pop phenomenon, who by his sheer physical presence, by his voice and gestures, produced a huge media sensation and had a powerful effect on people. Now, you do not have quite the same reputation or the same voice. Was that a problem for you?

I simply told myself that I am who I am. I don't try to be someone else. What I can give I give, and what I can't give I don't try to give, either. I don't try to make myself into something I am not. I am the person who happens to have been chosen—the cardinals are also to blame for that—and I do what I can.

World Youth Day, which drew 1.1 million participants to Cologne in August 2005, as well as the next World Youth Day in Sydney, brought to light unexpected qualities. As the left-leaning Italian newspaper La Repubblica *put it, "here on the Rhine", even his mistrustful countrymen had to admit that the armor of the watchdog of the faith was crumbling right before their eyes—to reveal a shepherd who described the Church as a "place of God's tenderness". Were you surprised by your own ability to relate so well to young people?*

At any rate I am happy that we have been able to establish such a spontaneous contact, and these Youth Days have actually turned out to be a genuine gift for me. When I think about the number of young people who experience these events as a fresh start, one that also sustains them spiritually after the events are over, or about the number of faith initiatives that get started or about the intense joy that remains and about the spirit of recollection that, amazingly, pervades the actual World Youth Days themselves, I cannot help saying: Something is happening here, and we are absolutely not the ones who are making it happen. In Australia, they had predicted huge security problems, difficulties and clashes, all the sorts of things that typically happen with mass demonstrations.

When it was all over, the police were enthusiastic, everyone was happy, because there had been absolutely no trouble at all. It was quite simply the common joy of faith that carried us through and that made it possible for hundreds of thousands of people to remain in silence before the Sacrament and so to become one. This spirit of recollection and gladness, this cheerfulness and authentic encounter, the absence of any crime—signs that something quite astonishing, something very different from other mass events, is truly happening here. And Sydney continues to bear fruit, for example, in priestly vocations. In the World Youth Days we have, I think, hit upon something that helps everyone.

With your soon to be twenty foreign visits, whether in Poland, the Czech Republic, Austria, Spain, Australia, North and South America, Africa, Portugal, Cyprus, Israel, or England, you have now become a traveling Pope yourself. Let's select just a few examples. In Brazil you visited some of the country's social service facilities and took part in the historic meeting of 176 cardinals and bishops from Latin America. You declared that the encounter between faith in God and the aboriginal peoples has for five hundred years animated and enlivened the countries of this continent. Yet today, you went on, the Catholic identity of the people is in jeopardy.

In the last twenty-five years, a huge shift has taken place in the religious geography. In countries or regions that before then still had up to 90 percent or more Catholics, the percentage has sunk to 60 percent. The change has two causes. On the one hand, Evangelical sects are plowing up the religious landscape—though they themselves are quite volatile in turn and are also incapable of generating any permanent sense of belonging. On the other hand, secularism has come to exercise a powerful influence through the media, and it is changing the way people think. In this sense, there is really a cultural crisis in Latin America, and it is a far-reaching one. This makes it all the more important for Catholicism to present its faith in a new and vital way and to reproclaim it as a force for unity, a force of solidarity and of eternity's openness to time.

During your trip to the US, the fallout from the abuse scandal occupied center stage. What kind of impression did you bring back with you from this visit?

I think even non-Catholics were surprised that the visit was not some kind of challenge, but that it revitalized the positive energies of the faith and touched everyone who was present. Wherever the Pope went, there were countless people, and there was a joy of being Catholic in the air that was quite incredible. Everywhere, whether in the magnificent liturgies—in Washington with more modern music, in New York it was typically classical—or else at the Catholic University, there was joyful participation, a sense of closeness, of communion, that touched me greatly. I also spoke with the abuse victims and became acquainted with many institutions that work with young people.

Has the Catholic Church in the United States already surmounted the crisis?

That might be an exaggeration, but, for one thing, it is aware of its fragility and of the problems and sin that are present in it. This is very important. In addition, there is an internal awakening to the need to overcome all these things and to live out and embody Catholic identity in new ways in our time.

You seem to have a very special love for Spain. You have already visited the country several times, and you will return there once more for World Youth Day 2011.

Spain is of course one of the great Catholic countries, and it has given the Church great saints and great bursts of creativity, and, in addition to that, it has also shaped the whole of Central and South America. Spain's history is always a fascinating subject, but the same thing is true precisely of its present as well. It is a land of dramatic contrasts. Think of the contrast between the Republic of the 1930s and Franco; or of the present dramatic struggle between radical secularity and resolute faith. It is a country that is still, as in the past, part of a major historical movement, plus it has a plurality of interacting cultures, for example, Basques and Catalonians. Spain has always been one of the great, creative Catholic countries, and—if, God willing, I am still alive—I will connect with it again, especially at World Youth Day in Madrid. Two small visits are planned for this year: one to the shrine of Saint James at Santiago de Compostela and another to the famous work of Gaudi, the Church of the Holy Family in Barcelona.

More people gather around the Pope in Spain than in any other country. This is astonishing when one considers the problems that the Catholic Church faces precisely in this land, problems that have to do in part with the failure to come to terms with the Franco dictatorship.

I would attribute that precisely to a vitality of faith that is apparently rooted in the DNA of the Spanish people.

France. Also a country with a great Catholic past, the origin of important religious orders, and the home of the unique shrine at

Lourdes, which you visited. But also a land with a very acute case of laicism.

Before my visit, people were saying that I was about to travel to a mostly atheist country where I would be greeted rather coldly. The opposite turned out to be the case. The liturgy in Paris was overwhelming. There were several thousand people gathered in the esplanade of the Church at Les Invalides—with an intensity of prayer and faith that was touching for me. Of course there was the unforgettable liturgy at Notre Dame, where the whole magnificent church was full of people simply immersed in prayer and the music was superb. The light and splendor of great French Catholic culture was on display there. Another fond recollection is the meeting with academics at the Institut de France and at the Collège des Bernardins, where I delivered a lecture that was attentively followed by the French intelligentsia, who accepted the Pope as somehow one of their own. Lourdes is of course a quite special place, where everything is full of faith, full of prayer, and where the Mother of God continues to be present and to touch and move people in an almost palpable manner. The anointing of the sick in Lourdes, which I administered to a group that included people facing imminent death and which took place in an atmosphere of humility and silent prayer, made a particularly powerful impression on me. It was very important for me to see that in so-called secular France the faith is not gone but is still present with an enormous energy.

Germany, of all places, is still waiting for an official visit from the German Pope, an anomalous situation, when you think about it. Is the reason for this situation a disgruntlement with the German government? Or displeasure with the spitefulness and small-minded anti-Roman attitudes that so often greet the Pope in the public discussion?

It is true that I have not yet visited Germany officially, but I have been there twice. I was once in Cologne, where I also met with the government, and once in Bavaria, which, don't forget, is actually a part of Germany as well. But you are right that the capital, too, has to be visited at some point. If the Lord grants me the strength, I would be very happy to visit Germany again.

Millions of people will rejoice, but at the same time they will respond by noting that it is late in the day, especially considering that the flock in the Pope's very own homeland is in such dire straits and stands in very urgent need of the shepherd's support.

Yes, the flock is in dire straits, and if I can come in person, I will do it gladly. Don't forget, though, that in the meantime I am also in lively contact with the shepherds and with so many other people in Germany, which means that there is, shall we say, a constant interior presence, and thus a very specific kind of closeness, on my part.

On the occasion of your trip to Africa in March 2009, the Vatican's policy on AIDS once again became the target of media criticism. Twenty-five percent of all AIDS victims around the world today are treated in Catholic facilities. In some countries, such as Lesotho, for example, the statistic is 40 percent. In Africa you stated that the Church's traditional teaching has proven to be the only sure way to stop the spread of HIV. Critics, including critics from the Church's own ranks, object that it is madness to forbid a high-risk population to use condoms.

The media coverage completely ignored the rest of the trip to Africa on account of a single statement. Someone had asked me why the Catholic Church adopts an unrealistic and ineffective position on AIDS. At that point, I really felt that I was being provoked, because the Church does more than anyone else. And I stand by that claim. Because she is the only institution that assists people up close and concretely, with prevention, education, help, counsel, and accompaniment. And because she is second to none in treating so many AIDS victims, especially children with AIDS.

I had the chance to visit one of these wards and to speak with the patients. That was the real answer: The Church does more than anyone else, because she does not speak from the tribunal of the newspapers, but helps her brothers and sisters where they are actually suffering. In my remarks I was not making a general statement about the condom issue, but merely said, and this is what caused such great offense, that we cannot solve the problem by distributing condoms. Much more needs to be done. We must stand close to the people, we must guide and help them; and we must do this both before and after they contract the disease.[1]

As a matter of fact, you know, people can get condoms when they want them anyway. But this just goes to show that condoms alone do not resolve the question itself. More needs to happen. Meanwhile, the secular realm itself has developed the so-called ABC Theory:

[1] The full text is in the appendix.

Abstinence-Be Faithful-Condom, where the condom is understood only as a last resort, when the other two points fail to work. This means that the sheer fixation on the condom implies a banalization of sexuality, which, after all, is precisely the dangerous source of the attitude of no longer seeing sexuality as the expression of love, but only a sort of drug that people administer to themselves. This is why the fight against the banalization of sexuality is also a part of the struggle to ensure that sexuality is treated as a positive value and to enable it to have a positive effect on the whole of man's being.

There may be a basis in the case of some individuals, as perhaps when a male prostitute uses a condom, where this can be a first step in the direction of a moralization, a first assumption of responsibility, on the way toward recovering an awareness that not everything is allowed and that one cannot do whatever one wants. But it is not really the way to deal with the evil of HIV infection. That can really lie only in a humanization of sexuality.

Are you saying, then, that the Catholic Church is actually not opposed in principle to the use of condoms?

She of course does not regard it as a real or moral solution, but, in this or that case, there can be nonetheless, in the intention of reducing the risk of infection, a first step in a movement toward a different way, a more human way, of living sexuality.

12. The Williamson Affair

*For the first four years, the Pope had been doing a "good job",
to put it colloquially. His opponents had literally been silenced.
But things changed in January 2009, and all at once the vicious
attacks started up again as well. A certain portion of the press
resurrected the charge that Pope Benedict is an ice-cold technocrat.
We touched on the event that triggered this reaction at the beginning of the interview: the lifting of the excommunication of four
bishops of the Society of Saint Pius X, which had broken off
from Rome under the French Archbishop Marcel Lefebvre. At
the present time, the Society comprises, according to its own account,
around 600,000 members, 500 priests, over 200 seminarians,
86 schools, and two institutions of higher education.*

*To start with: You must also have assumed that this step
would bring you anything but approval in the world of public
opinion, is that not right? The advantage to be gained was actually rather slight, whereas the risk of damage was considerable.*

That is correct. I have already explained that this step is
to a large extent parallel to what we are doing in China.
When bishops who are under excommunication because
they have offended against the primacy later acknowledge the primacy, they are justly freed from the excommunication. In other words, their excommunication had
nothing to do with Vatican II, as I have already said, but

had been pronounced on account of an offense against the primacy. But now they had written a letter declaring their Yes to the primacy, and the next step was therefore quite clear from a canonical point of view.

Incidentally, already under John Paul II an assembly of all the heads of the dicasteries, that is, all those in charge of Vatican bureaus, had decided to lift the excommunication in the event a letter of this kind was sent. Unfortunately, the public relations work was not done well from our side, so that the real, canonical substance and the limits of this process were never made clear. Then, to top it all off, there was the total meltdown with Williamson, which we had unfortunately not foreseen, and that is a particularly distressing circumstance.

Would you have signed the decree lifting the excommunication if you had known that among the four bishops there was a person who denied the existence of the Nazi gas chambers?

No. If I had known, the first step would have been to separate the Williamson case from the others. Unfortunately, though, none of us went on the Internet to find out what sort of person we were dealing with.

Shouldn't the very first step before lifting an excommunication have been to scrutinize the excommunicated persons and to examine carefully how they conducted their lives—especially when you were dealing with a community whose isolation had skewed its development in a direction that was both theologically and politically dubious?

It is correct that Williamson is an atypical case in that he was, when you think about, never Catholic in the proper sense. He was an Anglican and then went over directly to Lefebvre. This means that he has never lived in the great Church, that he has never lived with the Pope. Our offices that are in charge of dealing with these matters assured us that all four of the bishops were unreservedly ready to accept the primacy. But of course one is always more intelligent in hindsight.

Today one cannot help suspecting that the affair might have involved a plot aimed at inflicting the maximum possible damage on the Pope. The timing alone makes one suspect concerted action.[1]

In any case, the damage was massive. For weeks there was a hailstorm of negative headlines. And yet precisely one of the factors that made the affair possible in the first place was the hushing up of the facts. The Vatican press agency may not have done the best job, but the journalists in the employ of the major secular media did an even poorer one. One or two inquiries would have sufficed to clear things up. But no one wanted to spoil his own headlines about the scandal. As a matter of fact, the decree clearly explained that the Pope had decided only to "rethink" the canonical situation of the four bishops. It was clear that the four bishops would remain canonically suspended.

---

[1] The decree lifting the excommunication was dated January 21, 2009. It was pre-delivered to the Society on January 20. Precisely on January 21, that is, on the very day when the decree was already in the hands of the Society and was now irrevocable, Swedish television broadcast for the first time the fateful interview in which Williamson denied the existence of the Nazi gas chambers. But this interview had been prerecorded in November 2008. He had earlier stated that the Society can only be grateful for the "protection" it was currently afforded by the excommunication, which, he said, kept it safe from danger of contamination by the "neo-modernists" in the Vatican. Since it had not been aired until that point, no one in the Vatican could have had any idea of the statements it contained. It was not until the January 21 broadcast that this bomb was armed to go off. And by way of assurance that it would really go off, obviously willing journalists were specifically prepared for the sensational "firecracker".

They were forbidden to exercise their office. The step that had been taken did not mean a reconciliation, and it certainly did not mean a rehabilitation. And yet Germany's Süddeutsche Zeitung *published the devastating headline "Pope Rehabilitates Holocaust-Denier". Which the paper went on to call a shameful signal, indeed, a sinful lapse.*

How was it possible for your gesture to be understood as in any way a disavowal of reconciliation between Jews and Christians?

As I wrote in my letter afterward, we seem to be dealing here with a hostility, a readiness to pounce, that waits for these kinds of things to happen in order to strike a well-aimed blow. On our side, it was a mistake not to have studied and prepared the case more carefully. On the other hand, though, there was precisely, shall we say, a readiness for aggression, which was lying in wait for its victim.

All the leading offices in the Vatican immediately issued statements clarifying that Holocaust-deniers have no place in the Catholic Church. In fact, just two months earlier, on the ninth of November, you had recalled in Rome the seventieth anniversary of the Kristallnacht. *On that occasion you issued an appeal for "more profound solidarity with the Jewish world" and for prayer for the victims. You said that it is the duty of every individual to take up the fight on every level against every form of anti-Semitism and discrimination.*

At the general audience of January 28, 2009, your first opportunity to make a public personal statement regarding the Williamson affair, you read a declaration in which you expressed your "full and unquestionable solidarity with our fellow receivers of the First Covenant". You called the Shoah "a warning for all against forgetfulness, denial or reductionism" of the Holocaust.

Nevertheless, the General Secretary of the Central Council of Jews in Germany went so far as to claim that the Pope wanted to introduce a Holocaust-denier into "polite society". A Jewish journalist even spoke of rehabilitating active "Jew-haters". He called the Pope a "hypocrite". The President of the Central Council of Jews in Germany declared an immediate suspension of the dialogue with the Catholic Church. Doesn't all of this also suggest that, in light of the Williamson affair, the relation to the Jews is still in flux?

One thing that is evident, at any rate, is that there are still great fears and tensions and that the dialogue can easily be damaged and is fragile. In the worldwide Jewish community as a whole, however, there were many people who immediately vouched for me and said that I would never introduce a Holocaust-denier into polite society. These people know me. In that sense, a breakdown of the dialogue was out of the question.

The greatest danger of such a breakdown was in Germany, where there is evidently a very strong sensitivity and also a, let's say, vulnerability toward the Pope among Jews. It seems that the general image of the Pope among Germans has also affected the Jewish community, so that the statements you cite reflected not just the Jewish situation, but also the German situation in general. As was already said, it was of course a critical moment, which shows how vigilant we must be, how fragile the situation can be. At the same time, there was also always trust in the Jewish community worldwide.

Angela Merkel, the Protestant Chancellor of the country that was responsible for the Holocaust, called upon the Vatican to issue a clear denunciation of anti-Semitism, claiming that its previous statements in this regard were insufficient.

I do not want to rehearse all of that again. Apparently she was only imperfectly informed about what the Catholic Church had said and done before that point.

As you observed later, you found it especially saddening "that even Catholics, who, after all, might have had a better knowledge of the situation, thought they had to attack me".

In Catholic Germany there is a rather large group of people who, so to say, are on the lookout for an opportunity to attack the Pope; that is a fact, and it is one of the features of the face of Catholicism in our time. We must make a serious effort, we must struggle, to reestablish a basic accord.

Your trip to the Holy Land was slated for May 2009, a date that fell in the aftermath of the Williamson affair. The trip was now awaited with a great deal of nervous tension. Like your visit to Turkey, which took place immediately after the controversy ignited by the Regensburg address, your trip to the Holy Land produced an astounding change in the climate. Mordechay Lewy, the Israeli ambassador to the Holy See, declared that the relations between the Vatican and Israel had markedly improved. In that context, he cited a text from the biblical Book of Judges: "Out of the bitter came the sweet."

I have already remarked that the tension with Israel was not the same tension that existed in Germany. Rather, there was always a certain mutual trust. A knowledge that the Vatican stands by Israel, by the Jewish community around the world, that we acknowledge the Jews as our fathers and brothers. I was very moved by the kind of cordiality with which President Peres, who is a major figure, welcomed me. He himself of course is burdened with difficult memories. You know that they locked his father in a synagogue that they proceeded to set on fire. But he approached me with great openness and with the knowledge that we are struggling for common values and for peace, for the shaping of the future, and that the question of the existence of Israel plays an important role in that struggle.

On the whole I was met with great hospitality. I would say the security measures to protect me were almost excessive. In any case, the extent of the protection I was afforded was enormous. But we were able to do something that had not been possible with John Paul II, which was to celebrate two major public liturgies in Israel, a very beautiful one in Jerusalem and then, and this was very moving, in Nazareth, on the hill from which the crowd wanted to throw Jesus. That was a great, visible manifestation of Christian faith in the State of Israel.

And then of course it always goes to one's heart to visit the place where he preached, the place of his birth, the place of his Crucifixion, the tomb. These visits also gave me the chance to meet with the other Christian communities. These were all great and moving experiences. Finally, I also visited Jordan and the Palestinian Territory and was able to establish a very cordial relationship with the King of Jordan and the entire royal house. He made me a present of a hundred bottles of water from the Jordan, which he offered for use in baptisms.

In the autonomous Palestinian Territory there were powerful meetings with children whose parents were imprisoned in Israel. So we also saw the other side of the suffering, and in this way we got a broad, panoramic picture of the sufferings on both sides. This underscored even more clearly that nothing is solved by violence, that the only solution is peace, and that no effort should be spared to ensure that both sides in this tormented land can live in peace.

*

Let us look back at the first five years of your pontificate: What would be your provisional assessment of your time in office so far? What would you say you have already achieved, what seems particularly successful to you?

The major trips were important encounters with various cultures, and their effect endures; they were not some kind of show. When I think of Brazil, what a new beginning occurred in the meeting with the bishops! We started the continental mission, which is now truly shaping the diocesan programs in the country. Or take the meeting with *Fazenda da Esperança*, a drug rehabilitation center run by the good Father Hans Stapel, who is now overwhelmed by inquiries from people around the world wanting to start branches, which are now springing up all over the place. Everywhere one sensed the awareness that the Catholic Church is alive and full of energy. It was the same in the United States, in France, in Portugal. I think that the trips to the Czech Republic, to Austria, and to Poland, with that experience of vitality, were good. And the trip to Australia, of course, and to Africa, where there was a dynamism of joy that had a truly contagious effect. Every trip provided a chance for the Church to meet herself and, so, to meet the Lord, hence to become aware of herself before the Lord and to realize her provenance from him. Everywhere I went I was reminded of this again. So these and also other trips have been a kind of golden thread that has run through the pontificate so far and that has produced much fruit. On the other hand, there were the two years dedicated to major themes, the Year of Paul and the Year for Priests, with their respective points of emphasis. They enabled essential aspects of the faith to shine out with new light and to become topics for common reflection. The two synods, especially the Synod on the Word of God, were of great importance and were the scene of moving testimonies. On the other hand, we have had this long period of scandal and the wounds that have been inflicted on the Church, even though, as we have already said, they have a purifying virtue and so may turn out to be positive.

You once said that you must also "bear" this office, as it were. Are you also disappointed because certain things have not proved possible?

Of course I am also disappointed. By the continued existence of this lack of interest in the Church, especially in the Western world. By the fact that secularity continues to assert its independence and to develop in forms that increasingly lead people away from the faith. By the fact that the overall trend of our time continues to go against the Church. But I believe that this is just part of the

Christian situation, this battle between two kinds of love. The battle has always existed, and sometimes the one side and sometimes the other will be stronger.

Paul VI sold his tiara and gave away the proceeds. The last Pope to bear the name Benedict, Benedict XV, emptied the coffers after the First World War in order to give the money to the poor. Today, too, the world is waiting for convincing gestures from the Vatican; signs for all the world to see that the Church is serious about purifying herself and returning to the roots of the Apostolic Church. When will Benedict XVI put into action his statement that the Church has to separate herself from her goods in order to preserve her Good?

Those are words that Pius X used during the crisis in France, when the choice was between accepting the State system—which would have brought the Church certain advantages but, at the same time, would have subjected her to the State—or to renounce it and live in poverty. At that point, the Good was more important than goods. This is a criterion that is always valid and that we have to consult in every decision, especially also in the political decisions we make. But the point is not that we should carelessly throw away goods, so long as they retain their ancillary character. The question is how long a thing really serves the whole. It should never be the case that we become subject to it, so that then the goods dominate the Good, but rather the other way around.

At the moment it looks very much as if, after the first five-year period and in the wake of the abuses about which we have spoken, the pontificate of Benedict XVI has, if anything, become

*even more urgent, more resolute. You have even spoken of a
"new age of evangelization".*

Only time will tell what we will be able to do and achieve.
But we must summon fresh energy for tackling the problem of how to announce the gospel anew in such a way
that this world can receive it, and we must muster all of
our energies to do this. This is one of the points of the
program that I have received as my task.

PART III

WHERE DO WE GO FROM HERE?

13. Church, Faith, and Society

Society's problems have not gotten any better, and this under-scores all the more the urgency of the questions concerning the shape we should give our lives: What are our values and standards? What are we actually doing with our lives? How do we want to live them in the future? We see in our time a world in danger of sliding into the abyss. We see an unrestrained economic system ready to mutate into a predatory capitalism that devours values on a huge scale; we see that life in the fast lane is not only beyond our means, but that it also robs us of our moral compass; we see the growth of a society that plunges ahead restlessly, and with no clear sense of direction, regarding today as wrong what yesterday was still considered right and regarding tomorrow as right what today is still considered wrong.

We have illnesses such as burnout, now a mass phenomenon, and new addictions to things such as video games and pornography. We have the almost unmanageable work-related stress produced by the mania for profit maximization that drives the business world. We have the precarious situation of children who suffer on account of the loss of family relations. We have the dominance of the media, which have developed a culture bent on breaking our taboos, dumbing us down, and blunting our moral sense. We have the offerings of the electronic media, which have the potential to manipulate and destroy the qualities that make us human.

Holy Father, the Church's contribution to the development of civilization has always been of great relevance. Today, however, an attitude of contempt for and, with increasing frequency, even of hostility toward the Christian religion is spreading in many countries. What has happened?

First of all, the development of the modern idea of progress and science has created a mentality that we think will make the "God hypothesis" superfluous, as Laplace put it. Today man thinks that he himself can do everything that he once awaited from God alone. In light of this would-be scientific intellectual model, matters of faith appear as archaic, as mythical, as belonging to a bygone civilization. Religion, at least the Christian religion, is accordingly classified as a relic of the past. As early as the eighteenth century, the Enlightenment was announcing that the Pope, that the Dalai Lama of Europe, was inevitably doomed to disappear one day. The Enlightenment, it was thought, would finally sweep away these mythological holdovers once and for all.

Are we dealing with an authority problem rooted in the fact that a liberal society is no longer willing to listen to any voice other than its own? Or is there also a problem of communication, in that the Church is no longer able to convey her traditional values using concepts such as sin, repentance, and conversion?

I would say that it is both. This way of thinking, which has such a record of success and contains much that is correct, has changed man's basic orientation toward reality. He no longer seeks the mystery, the divine, but is convinced that science will at some point decipher everything that at present we do not yet understand. It is only a matter of time before we have dominion over everything. In this way, science became the supreme category without qualification. I recently had to laugh at a statement on television to the effect that it has now been scientifically demonstrated that it is useful for children for their mothers to show them affection. One might regard such studies as silliness or as the expression of a vulgarized and infantile pseudo-concept of science, but this concept also indicates a pattern. By which I mean precisely a kind of thinking in which faith in the mystery, in the working of God, the whole religious dimension, is regarded as "unscientific" and so has been invalidated and ruled out. That is one side of the question.

And the other side?

The other side is that precisely science itself is now regaining an insight into its limits, that many scientists today are saying: "Doesn't everything have to come from somewhere?" and that we have to pose this question again. A new understanding of religion is reemerging because of this. An understanding of religion, not as a mythical, archaic phenomenon, but as one that emerges from the intrinsic coherence of the logos—which is exactly the real faith in the gospel that the gospel itself sought and proclaimed.

But, as I have already said, religiosity has to regenerate itself anew in this large context—and in doing so also find new forms for its expression and comprehension. People today no longer have an immediate intuitive grasp of the fact that Christ's blood on the Cross is expiation for their sins. Formulas like these are great and true, but they no longer have a place in our overall system of thought and world view; they stand in need of new translation and comprehension. For example, we have to recover the understanding that it really is necessary to come to terms with evil. We cannot simply shove it aside or forget it. It has to be worked through and transformed from within.

What does that mean?

It means that we really are in an age in which a new evangelization is needed; in which the one gospel has to be proclaimed both in its great, enduring rationality and in its power that transcends rationality, so that it can reenter our thinking and understanding in a new way.

Of course, man always remains the same, no matter how much he changes. There would not be so many believers unless people still understood in their hearts: Yes, what religion tells us is what we need. Science alone, in its self-isolating search for autonomy, does not do justice to the whole range of our life. It is a sector that gives us great gifts, but it depends in turn on man's remaining man.

We have seen it ourselves: progress has increased our capabilities, but not our moral and human stature and capacity. We have to regain an internal balance, and we also need spiritual growth. This is something that the tribulations of our time are increasingly teaching us to recognize.

Before we discuss the problems and future of the Catholic Church, I would like to ask what the Church, which you once defined as a "spiritual organism", actually is in the first place. In one of your homilies, you cited a passage from Paul VI, who said that he loved the Church so intensely that he always "wished to embrace, greet, and love" her. The Pope went on to say: "I would finally like to understand her in every aspect: in her history, in her divine plan of salvation, in her definitive destiny, in her complexity." Paul VI concluded with the words: "mysterious body of Christ".

Paul VI was going back to what Saint Paul had developed when he defined the Church as Christ's permanent bodiliness, as the living organism of Christ. Paul understood the Church precisely not as an institution, as an organization, but as a living organism, in which all the members work with and in relation to each other, in which they are all united because of Christ. This is an image, but it is an image that leads deep below the surface and that is very realistic, if for no other reason than because we believe that in the Eucharist we really receive Christ, the Risen One. And if every member receives the same Christ, then we are all really gathered in this new, risen body as the locus of a new humanity. It is important to understand this and so to conceive the Church, not as an organization that is supposed to perform every possible function—the organization is part of the larger picture, but it has to remain limited—but as a living organism that comes from Christ himself.

In many countries, there are lay initiatives devoted more to fighting for independence from Rome and for the establishment of a local church that is both national and democratic in character. The Vatican is portrayed in this context as a dictatorship, and the Pope is presented as using authoritarian means to push through his own positions. If one looks more closely at the situation, one notices that it is the centrifugal, rather than the centripetal, forces that are gaining in strength and more the rebellion against Rome that is becoming more powerful than solidarity with Rome. Hasn't the by now decades-old battle for the direction of the Church long since brought about a sort of schism within the Catholic Church as well?

First of all, I would say that the Pope has no coercive power. His "power" exists only to the extent that there is conviction, that people realize that we belong together and the Pope has a task that he has not given himself. It is only when there is conviction that the whole enterprise can succeed. Only through the conviction of the common faith can the Church maintain a common life. I receive so many letters, both from simple people and from prominent personages, who write to tell me "We are one with the Pope, for us he is the Vicar of Christ and the Successor of Peter; be assured that we believe and live in communion with you." Of course there are centrifugal forces, and there always have been; they weren't invented yesterday. There has always been a tendency toward national churches, and in fact some have actually been founded. Yet precisely today, in a globalized society, in our need for the world community to have an interior unity, it is becoming evident that these tendencies are actually anachronisms. It is becoming clear that a Church does not grow by withdrawing into some national shell, by separating herself, by shutting herself up in a certain culture and absolutizing it, but that the Church needs unity, that she needs something like a primacy.

It was interesting for me that the Russian Orthodox theologian John Meyendorff, who lives in America, said that their autocephalies[1] are their biggest problem; they

---

[1] Autocephaly is originally a Greek term referring to self-determination. In the Orthodox Church, it is a word used to designate an autonomous Church. Autocephalies are governed by their own supreme head and choose their archbishops or metropolitans themselves.

could use something like a first authority, a primate. This is said in other communities, too. The problems of non-Catholic Christendom are largely caused, both theologically and pragmatically, by the fact that they have no organ of unity. So this situation also makes evident the need for an organ of unity, which of course acts, not dictatorially, but out of the interior communion of the faith. The centrifugal tendencies will continue to exist, of course, but the development of history, the arrow in which history moves, tells us that the Church needs an organ of unity.

In the last decades, many dioceses have tried almost every pastoral experiment in an effort to "modernize" the Church. This has garnered the criticism of German philosopher Rüdiger Safranski, who says that Christianity has become a "cold religious project", a "mix of social ethics, institutional power thinking, psychotherapy, techniques of meditation, museum curation, cultural project management, and social work". Critics observe that a widespread desire to be like everyone else has robbed ordinary Catholics of their awareness that faith grows from roots entirely different from those of the pleasure-oriented societies of the West. In the meantime, however, so many theologians and priests have themselves gone so far off the rails that it's only with great difficulty that we can still discern a Catholic profile anywhere.

What went wrong?

Well, it has to do with the forces of disintegration that are present in the human soul. An additional factor is the urge to win public acceptance; or else to discover some island where there is virgin soil and we still have a chance to shape things independently. The development then takes either one of two directions. Either one engages in political moralism, as happened in liberation theology and in other experiments, as a way of giving Christianity what you might call a relevance for the present. Or there is a transformation in the direction of psychotherapy and wellness, in other words, of forms where religion is identified with my possession of some sort of holistic well-being. All of these attempts come from having set aside the real root, faith. What is left—as your citations correctly describe—are self-made projects. They may have a limited vitality, but they do not establish any communion with God worthy of the name and are also incapable of binding men together in any enduring fashion. They are islands where only certain people settle, and these islands are short-lived, since fashions obviously change.

There is a question that we have to ask in this connection. How is it possible that in many Western countries every child spends years studying the Catholic religion in school, yet on graduation may know more about Buddhism than he does about the basic tenets of Catholicism, which he may not even be able to recognize? All of which happens in a system that is under the responsibility of the dioceses.

That is a question that I also ask myself. Every child in Germany has nine to thirteen years of religion in school. Why, in spite of that, so very little sticks, if I may put it like that, is incomprehensible. You are right that the bishops must seriously reflect on ways to give catechesis a new heart and a new face.

A "culture of doubt" is very much "in" these days, and it has found a comfortable nest even in media outlets associated with the Church. In many cases, editors simply take over uncritically the slogans circulating among the usual critics of the Church. Bishops follow the lead of their media consultants, who recommend a soft line in order to avoid any damage to the bishops' liberal image. And when, on top of that, huge media concerns belonging to the Church remove religious books from their main sales lists—doesn't this raise doubts as to whether we can still speak credibly about new evangelization?

These are all phenomena that one can only observe with sadness. It is sad that there are what you might call professional Catholics who make a living on their Catholicism, but in whom the spring of faith flows only faintly, in a few scattered drops. We must really make an effort to change this. In Italy—where there are far fewer enterprises run by the Church as an institution—I observe that initiatives arise, not because they are set up by the Church as institution, but because the people themselves believe. Spontaneous new beginnings arise, not from institutions, but out of an authentic faith.

The Church must always be in movement; she is permanently "underway". Doesn't the Pope wonder sometimes whether many of the things he resists cannot be stopped because they simply reflect the necessary process of civilization, with which the Church cannot refuse to go along?

Of course we always need to ask what are the things that may once have been considered essential to Christianity but in reality were only the expression of a certain period. What, then, is really essential? This means that we must constantly return to the gospel and the teachings of the faith in order to see: First, what is an essential component? Second, what legitimately changes with the changing times? And third, what is not an essential component? In the end, then, the decisive point is always to achieve the proper discernment.

14. Overdue Reforms?

Celibacy, women's ordination, homosexuality—for decades now, this unchanging canon of issues has dominated discussion in the media. Only a positive resolution of these questions, so the thinking goes, will allow the Church to regain her attractiveness. It is striking that the Lutheran Church in Germany—without celibacy and with women's ordination—is losing more members than the Catholic Church. On the other hand, it is also true that these positions make the proclamation of the faith harder. Can we briefly go through a few points one by one?

Catholics who remarry after a divorce are barred from receiving communion. You once remarked that this regulation would require "more intense reflection".

Of course that is required. On the one hand, there is the certainty that the Lord tells us that a marriage contracted in faith is indissoluble. These are words we cannot manipulate. We have to let them stand as they are—even when they contradict the forms of life that are dominant today. There were epochs in which what was Christian prevailed to such an extent that the indissolubility of marriage was the norm, but in many civilizations it is not the norm. Bishops from Third World countries tell me time and again that "the sacrament of marriage is the hardest one." Or else: "In our country it is still not popular." To bring traditional forms of cohabitation into alignment with the sacrament of matrimony is a process that is bound up with the whole of existence, and it is a struggle whose outcome cannot be coerced. In this sense, what we are experiencing in the midst of the gradual disintegration of Western society is not the only crisis in question. But that is no reason to give up monogamous marriage or to cease struggling to preserve this form. That would contradict the gospel.

Jesus tells us that the Creator made human beings male and female and that what God has joined, no man may put asunder. But the first disciples already murmured at this commandment.

Yes. One thing we can do is inquire more precisely into the question of the validity of marriages. Up to now, canon law has taken it for granted that someone who contracts a marriage knows what marriage is. Assuming the existence of this knowledge, the marriage is then valid and indissoluble. But in the present confusion of opinions, in today's completely new situation, what people "know" is rather that divorce is supposedly normal. So we have to deal with the question of how to recognize validity and where healing is possible. This will always remain a struggle. But that is no reason not to maintain the standard or to capitulate. That would not raise the moral level of society. Preserving this difficult teaching as a standard by which people can continue to measure themselves is a necessary task to prevent further disasters.

There is, then, a certain tension in the thing itself. Pastoral care, for its part, has to seek ways of staying close to individuals and of helping them, even in, shall we say, their irregular situation, to believe in Christ as the Savior, to believe in his goodness, because he is always there for them, even though they cannot receive communion. And of helping them to remain in the Church, even though their situation is canonically irregular. Pastoral care has to help them accept that, yes, I do not live up to what I should be as a Christian, but I do not cease to be a Christian, to be loved by Christ, and the more I remain in the Church, the more I am sustained by him.

Paul VI made the topic of contraception the theme of his famous 1968 encyclical Humanae vitae. *At that time, he pointed out that man's attempt to manipulate the natural order leads to fatal consequences. Life, Pope Paul said, is too great, too sacred, for us to meddle in it. It is as if to say: If we do not respect the lives of children, our own lives and the life of our society, our world, will be lost. Perhaps people at the time were not yet able to understand this vision. Today we are witnessing not only the enormously injurious consequences of the contraceptive pill on human health and on the environment, but we are also watching our social systems collapse because we have become a childless society that is losing its foundations. Nevertheless, it has become almost impossible for the Catholic Church even to make her sexual ethics understandable. A supermodel from Brazil recently said, as if to prove our point, that nowadays no woman enters marriage as a virgin. A retired auxiliary bishop has criticized the Church for answering the questions pertaining to premarital sexuality in such a way that "practically no one can live them and people doubtless live them quite differently."*

This is a huge question. Given the present framework, we cannot enter into the many layers of the problem or examine the issues in detail. It is correct there is much in this area that needs to be pondered and expressed in new ways. On the other hand, I would also disagree with the supermodel, and many others as well, and I would insist that statistics do not suffice as a criterion for morality. It is bad enough when public opinion polls become the criterion of political decisions and when politicians are more preoccupied with "How do I get more votes?" than with "What is right?" By the same token, the results of surveys about what people do or how they live is not in and of itself the measure of what is true and right.

Paul VI has been proved prophetically right. He was convinced that society robs itself of its greatest hopes when it kills human beings through abortion. How many children are killed who might one day have been geniuses, who could have given humanity something new, who could have given us a new Mozart or some new technical discovery? We need to stop and think about the great human capacity that is being destroyed here—even quite apart from the fact that unborn children are human persons whose dignity and right to life we have to respect.

The contraceptive pill is another problem in its own right.

Yes. What Paul VI wanted to say, and what is still correct as a main vision, is that if we separate sexuality and fecundity from each other in principle, which is what the use of the pill does, then sexuality becomes arbitrary. Logically, every form of sexuality is of equal value. This approach to fecundity as something apart from sexuality, so far apart that we may even try to produce children rationally and no longer see them as a natural gift, was, after all, quickly followed by the ascription of equal value to homosexuality.

The basic lines of *Humanae vitae* are still correct. Finding ways to enable people to live the teaching, on the other hand, is a further question. I think that there will always be core groups of people who are really open to being interiorly convinced and fulfilled by the teaching and who then carry everyone else. We are sinners. But we should not take the failure to live up to this high moral standard as an authoritative objection to the truth. We should try to do as much good as we can and to support and put up with each other. We should also try to express the teaching pastorally, theologically, and intellectually in the context of today's studies of sexuality and anthropology so as to create the conditions for understanding so that people can realize that this is a great task on which work is being done and on which even more and better work needs to be done.

You can count on support from at least one former Hollywood star and sex symbol, Raquel Welch, who now says that the introduction of the contraceptive pill fifty years ago has led to sex without responsibility. She added that it weakens marriage and family and leads to "situations of chaos". But does the Catholic Church in point of fact refuse any regulation of conception whatsoever?

No. After all, everyone knows that the Church affirms natural regulation of conception, which is not just a method, but also a way of life. Because it presupposes that couples take time for each other. And that is something fundamentally different from when I take the pill without binding myself interiorly to another person, so that I can jump into bed with a random acquaintance.

The fact that only Catholics are allowed to participate in the Eucharist is understood as a form of exclusion, by many even as a form of discrimination. We cannot talk about the unity of Christians, it is objected, if we are not even prepared to celebrate Jesus' legacy together at the altar. What does the Pope have to say about this?

The Catholic Church is not alone in teaching that only someone who belongs completely to her in faith can receive the Eucharist. This is also the teaching of Orthodoxy around the world. Both the New Testament and the Apostolic Fathers make it unmistakably clear that the Eucharist is the most intimate heart of the Church—life in the body of Christ in the one communion. This is why the Eucharist is not just some social ritual where people meet in an amicable way; rather, it is the expression of being in the center of the Church. It therefore cannot be detached from this condition of belonging—for the very simple reason that the Eucharist is this act of belonging itself.

It always seems that celibacy is to blame for everything, whether it's sexual abuse, the exodus from the Church, or the priest shortage. Regarding the last point, we should perhaps say that there are more, not fewer, priests today in proportion to the number of those who attend Mass. In Germany, at least, there are actually twice as many priests in relation to Catholics who still practice their faith than there were in 1960. And yet we have reached a point where even bishops recommend that we exercise "the imagination" needed to "enable the service of married men as priests alongside the basic form of celibate priesthood".

I can certainly understand that bishops would reflect on that, given the confusion of the times. But things get complicated when it comes time to say what such coexistence of the two forms would actually be supposed to look like. I believe that celibacy becomes a very meaningful sign, and above all becomes possible to live, when priests begin to form communities. It is important for priests not to live off on their own somewhere, in isolation, but to accompany one another in small communities, to support one another, and so to experience, and constantly realize afresh, their communion in service to Christ and in renunciation for the sake of the Kingdom of heaven.

Celibacy is always, shall we say, an affront to what man normally thinks. It is something that can only be done, and is only credible, if there is a God and if celibacy is my doorway into the Kingdom of God. In this sense, celibacy is a special kind of sign. The scandal that it provokes consists precisely in the fact that there are people who believe these things. By the same token, this scandal has a positive side.

The impossibility of women's ordination in the Catholic Church has been clearly decided by a "non possumus" of the supreme Magisterium. The Congregation for the Doctrine of the Faith laid this down under Paul VI in the 1976 document Inter insigniores, and John Paul II reinforced it in his 1994 apostolic letter Ordinatio sacerdotalis. In this document, speaking in virtue of his office about the "divine constitution of the Church", he writes—and these are his exact words—"that the Church has no authority whatsoever to confer priestly ordination on women and that this judgment is to be definitively held by all the Church's faithful". Critics see this as a form of discrimination. The only reason Jesus did not call women to be priestesses, it is said, is that this would have been unthinkable two thousand years ago.

That is nonsense, since the world was full of priestesses at the time. All religions had their priestesses, and the astonishing thing was actually that they were absent from the community of Jesus Christ, a fact that in turn is a point of continuity with the faith of Israel.

John Paul II's formulation is very important: The Church has "no authority" to ordain women. The point is not that we are saying that we don't *want* to, but that we *can't*. The Lord gave the Church a form with the Twelve and, as their successors, with the bishops and the presbyters, the priests. This form of the Church is not something we ourselves have produced. It is how he constituted the Church. Following this is an act of obedience. This obedience may be arduous in today's situation. But it is important precisely for the Church to show that we are not a regime based on arbitrary rule. We cannot do what we want. Rather, the Lord has a will for us, a will to which we adhere, even though doing so is arduous and difficult in this culture and civilization. Incidentally, women have so many great and meaningful functions in the Church that there can be no question of discrimination. That would be the case if the priesthood were a sort of dominion, whereas it is actually intended to be pure service. If you look at the history of the Church, women—from Mary to Monica and all the way down to Mother Teresa—have so eminent a significance that in many respects they shape the image of the Church more than men do. Just think of major Catholic feast days such as Corpus Christi or Mercy Sunday, which originated with women. In Rome, for example, there is even a Church where not a single man can be seen in any of the altarpieces.

Homosexual practice has the status of a widely accepted form of life in the West today. Modernists even publicize its approval as a measure of a given society's degree of progress. In the Catechism of the Catholic Church, *which was promulgated under your responsibility as Prefect of the Congregation for the Doctrine of the Faith, we read that "the number of men and women who have deep-seated homosexual tendencies is not negligible.... They must be accepted with respect, compassion, and sensitivity. Every sign of unjust discrimination in their regard should be avoided. These persons are called to fulfill God's will in their lives." And yet the same Catechism contains the following statement: "Basing itself on Sacred Scripture, which presents homosexual acts as acts of grave depravity, tradition has always declared that homosexual acts are intrinsically disordered." Doesn't this second statement somewhat contradict the respect for homosexuals expressed in the first one?*

No. It is one thing to say that they are human beings with their problems and their joys, that as human beings they deserve respect, even though they have this inclination, and must not be discriminated against because of it. Respect for man is absolutely fundamental and decisive.

At the same time, though, sexuality has an intrinsic meaning and direction, which is not homosexual. We could say, if we wanted to put it like this, that evolution has brought forth sexuality for the purpose of reproducing the species. The same thing is true from a theological point of view as well. The meaning and direction of sexuality is to bring about the union of man and woman and, in this way, to give humanity posterity, children, a future. This is the determination internal to the essence of sexuality. Everything else is against sexuality's intrinsic meaning and direction. This is a point we need to hold firm, even if it is not pleasing to our age.

The issue at stake here is the intrinsic truth of sexuality's significance in the constitution of man's being. If someone has deep-seated homosexual inclinations—and it is still an open question whether these inclinations are really innate or whether they arise in early childhood—if, in any case, they have power over him, this is a great trial for him, just as other trials can afflict other people as well. But this does not mean that homosexuality thereby becomes morally right. Rather, it remains contrary to the essence of what God originally willed.

It is no secret that there are homosexuals even among priests and monks. Just recently there was a major scandal on account of the homosexual passions of priests in Rome.

Homosexuality is incompatible with the priestly vocation. Otherwise, celibacy itself would lose its meaning as a renunciation. It would be extremely dangerous if celibacy became a sort of pretext for bringing people into the priesthood who don't want to get married anyway. For, in the end, their attitude toward man and woman is somehow distorted, off center, and, in any case, is not within the direction of creation of which we have spoken. The Congregation for Education issued a decision a few years ago to the effect that homosexual candidates cannot become priests because their sexual orientation estranges them from the proper sense of paternity, from the intrinsic nature of priestly being. The selection of candidates to the priesthood must therefore be very careful. The greatest attention is needed here in order to prevent the intrusion of this kind of ambiguity and to head off a situation where the celibacy of priests would practically end up being identified with the tendency to homosexuality.

But there is no doubt that homosexuality exists in monasteries and among the clergy, if not acted out, then at least in a nonpracticed form.

Well, that is just one of the disturbing problems of the Church. And the persons who are affected must at least try not to express this inclination actively, in order to remain true to the intrinsic mission of their office.

The Catholic Church sees herself as the locus of God's unique revelation. She claims to give expression to God's message, which raises man to his highest dignity, goodness, and beauty. The only problem is that this is increasingly hard to convey to people nowadays, especially when you consider the quantity of what you might call competitors in the religion market. During a meeting with artists in Lisbon, you said that the "dialogue with the world" involved a coexistence of truths.

It is not the same thing to say that Christ is the Son of God in whom the full presence of the truth about God finds expression and to say that various kinds of truths are also present in other religions, that they have something like fragments, or beams of the great light, that, in a certain respect, they even represent an inner movement toward him. The claim that God is present in Christ and that the true God himself thus appears and speaks to us in him does not rule out that the other religions also contains truths—but that is just the point: truths that, as it were, point to *the* Truth. In this sense, dialogue, which is meant to make reference to him evident, is an intrinsic consequence of the situation of humanity.

15. How Is the Church Renewed?

Holy Father, no one will dispute that the Church is in need of purification and renewal, especially after the most recent abuse scandals. The only question is: What exactly is real renewal, the right kind of renewal? You have used dramatic words to show clearly that the destiny of the faith and the Church is decided solely "in the context of the liturgy". An outsider might think that it is more a secondary question which words are spoken at Mass or which bodily postures are used or which actions are performed.

The Church becomes visible for people in many ways, in charitable activity or in missionary projects, but the place where the Church is actually experienced most of all as Church is the liturgy. And that is also as it should be. At the end of the day, the point of the Church is to turn us toward God and to enable God to enter into the world. The liturgy is the act in which we believe that *he* enters our lives and that we touch him. It is the act in which what is really essential takes place: We come into contact with God. He comes to us—and we are illumined by him.

The liturgy gives us strength and guidance in two forms. On the one hand, we hear His Word, which means that we really hear him speaking and receive his instruction about the path we should follow. On the other hand, he gives himself to us in the transformed bread. Of course, the words can always differ, the bodily attitudes can differ. The Eastern Church, for instance, uses certain gestures that differ from the ones familiar to us. In India, the same gestures that they share with us have a partly different significance. The essential point is that the Word of God and the reality of the Sacrament really occupy center stage; that we don't bury God underneath our words and our ideas and that the liturgy doesn't turn into an occasion to display ourselves.

So liturgy is something that is given in advance?

Yes. It is not about our doing something, about our demonstrating our creativity, in other words, about displaying everything we can do. Liturgy is precisely not a show, a piece of theater, a spectacle. Rather, it gets its life from the Other. This has to become evident, too. This is why the fact that the ecclesial form has been given in advance is so important. It can be reformed in matters of detail, but it cannot be reinvented every time by the community. It is not a question, as I said, of self-production. The point is to go out of and beyond ourselves, to give ourselves to him, and to let ourselves be touched by him.

In this sense, it's not just the expression of this form that's important, but also its communality. This form can exist in different rites, but it must always contain that element which precedes us, that comes from the whole of the Church's faith, from the whole of her tradition, from the whole of her life, and does not just spring from the fashion of the moment.

Are you saying that we have to remain in a state of passivity?

No. Because it's precisely this approach, you see, that really challenges us to let ourselves be snatched out of the mere momentary situation; to enter into the totality of the faith, to understand it, to take part in it interiorly, and, on that basis, to give the liturgy the worthy form that makes it beautiful and a source of joy. Now that is exactly what happened in a very special way in Bavaria—for example, through the great flowering of Church music or else the efflorescence of joy in the Bavarian Rococo. Of course it is important that we give the whole a beautiful form, but always in the service of what precedes us, and not as something that we ourselves are first supposed to produce.

You have stated that, when it comes to the holiness of the Eucharist, there is no room for alternatives. The Eucharist, you say, is the hinge on which all renewal turns. The very possibility of spiritual revolutions depends on the spirit of the Eucharist.

If it is true—as we believe it is—that Christ is really present in the Eucharist, then this is the event that is at the center of absolutely everything. It is the event, not just of a single day, but of the history of the world as a whole, as the decisive force that then becomes the source from which changes can come. The important point is that the Lord's Word and his real presence in the signs are inseparable in the Eucharist. It is important that we also receive instruction in the Word. That we answer through our prayer and that God's guidance, our following, and our allowing ourselves to be changed thus form an interlocking whole—so that men themselves can be changed, which is the most important precondition for any really positive change in the world.

If we want the world to move forward a little, the only criterion in terms of which this can happen is God, who enters into our lives as a real presence. The Eucharist is the place where men can receive the kind of formation from which new things come into being. This is why the great figures who throughout history have really brought about revolutions for the good have been the saints who, touched by Christ, have brought new impulses into the world.

In the eleventh chapter, the conciliar document Lumen Gentium *describes Sunday participation in the Eucharistic sacrifice as the "source and summit of the entire Christian life". Christ says: "He who eats my flesh and drinks my blood has eternal life." As Pope, you have begun to administer communion on the tongue, while the communicants receive the sacrament on their knees. Do you regard this as the appropriate posture?*

The first point that needs to be made is that time has a structure that is common for all believers. The Old Testament prescribes this structure already in light of the creation account, presenting the Sabbath as the day when God rests and men rest with him. For Christians, time gets this structure from Sunday, the day of the Resurrection, when he encounters us and we encounter him. Once again, the most important act here is, as it were, the moment when he unites himself to us through his self-gift.

I am not opposed in principle to communion in the hand; I have both administered and received communion in this way myself. The idea behind my current practice of having people kneel to receive communion on the tongue was to send a signal and to underscore the real presence with an exclamation point. One very important reason is that there is a great danger of superficiality precisely in the kinds of mass events we hold at Saint Peter's, both in the Basilica and in the Square. I have heard of people who, after receiving communion, stick the Host in their wallet to take home as a kind of souvenir. In this context, where people think that everyone is just automatically supposed to receive communion—everyone else is going up, so I will, too—I wanted to send a clear signal. I wanted it to be clear: Something quite special is going on here! *He* is here, the One before whom we fall on our knees! Pay attention! This is not just some social ritual in which we can take part if we want to.

Mary is the God-bearer. In a certain sense, she brings God into the world. Is this an image, mutatis mutandis, *of what all Christians should be: God-bearers?*

At a certain point, they said to the Lord: "Behold, your mother and your brothers and sisters are outside." Indicating the people gathered around him, he said "He who does the will of my Father is mother, brother, and sister to me." In saying this, he also transmitted the mission of maternity to us, so that we might, as it were, give God a new chance to be born in our time, too. The birth of God was one of the major themes for the Church Fathers. They said that God was born once in Bethlehem, but that there is also a very significant and profound way in which he must be born again in every new generation, and it is to this, they thought, that every Christian is called.

Shouldn't we rate Jesus' contribution to the liberation of women, who were largely excluded from access to religion, to God, and to society, at least as highly as the opening of God's revelation to the Gentiles?

It is correct that Jesus brought women into a closer relationship with him than had been thinkable before his time and that, after the Resurrection, he made a woman the first witness, which means that women were welcomed into the innermost circle of his friends, something that indeed signaled a new shift. From the point of view of comparative religion, though, I would be cautious about saying that this was some kind of immediate explosion. There was a gradual unfolding. But it is an important fact, as you say, that Jesus gave women access to a whole new position in the community of faith, first, by making his Mother the Mother of Christians under the Cross and, second, by granting his first post-Resurrection appearance to a woman.

In the West, the Roman Church is in the throes of a massive, unprecedented change, especially in terms of numbers. In the next ten years, for example, the current number of laity, priests, and religious in Germany will drop by a third. Of the approximately 24,000 women religious alive today, about 80 percent are older than sixty-five. The same percentages hold for monks and priests as well. Churches have to be closed, parishes combined. The folk church will continue to dwindle. As early as 1971, you suggested that the Church will "shrink and will to a large extent have to restart entirely from the beginning". The Church, you said, will no longer be able to fill many of the places of worship that were built during the boom, and, as the number of members declines, the Church will also lose many of her social privileges. Many observers claim that the only thing left of the folk church is a "management of practical unbelief". But criterion for the Church cannot, it is said, be outward success. For when it is above all a matter of the quantity of believers, then it is less the substance of the faith than the mere fact of showing up in church that occupies center stage.

Is the folk church on its way out?

When you look at the world as a whole, the answer varies greatly from place to place. In many parts of the world, there never was a folk church to begin with. In Japan, Christians are a tiny minority. In Korea, they are an expanding, vital force, which even has an influence on public opinion, but they are not a folk church. In the Philippines there is a folk church, and even today a *Filipino* is simply a Catholic—with joy and with exuberance. In India, as in Japan, Christians are a marginal minority, though they have a significant social role, which is in turn a contentious issue in an Indian society that recognizes Hinduism as its identity.

As was just said, the situation, on a global scale, is quite varied. It is true, though, that, in the Western world, the identification of folk and Church is melting away. In the Eastern part of Germany, this process is already quite far advanced. There, the unbaptized are already in the majority. And in the same way, the number of Christians in large parts of the Western world is on the decline. Nevertheless, there is still a cultural identity shaped by Christianity that people also wish to retain. I recall a French politician who described himself as a "Protestant atheist". By that he meant, I may be an atheist, but I know that my cultural roots are planted in the soil of Protestantism.

That makes things complicated.

Yes, because the Christian origins are still part of the broad cultural climate of many Western countries. But we are heading increasingly toward a form of Christianity based on personal decision. And it will decide in turn the extent to which the general Christian character remains at work. I would say that the task today is, on the one hand, to consolidate, enliven, and enlarge this Christianity of personal decision, so that more people can consciously live and profess their faith again. On the other hand, we have to acknowledge that we are not simply identical with the nation as such—and yet that we have the energy to impress upon it, and present to it, values that it can accept, even when the majority are not believing Christians.

16. Mary and the Message of Fatima

Unlike your predecessor, you are regarded as a theologian who focuses more on Jesus than on Mary. Yet already a month after your election, you called upon the faithful gathered in Saint Peter's Square to entrust themselves to Our Lady of Fatima. You made some sensational remarks when you visited Fatima in May 2010. You said that the event that took place ninety-three years ago in Fatima, when the heavens opened above Portugal, should be thought of "as a window of hope" that God opens "when man closes the door to him". The very Pope who is known to the world as the defender of reason was now saying that "the Virgin Mary came from heaven to remind us of Gospel truths."

It is true that I grew up with a primarily Christocentric piety of the sort that had developed between the two world wars through the reawakened interest in the Bible and the Fathers. This was a piety that fed very consciously and decidedly on the Bible and that, as the name suggests, focuses on Christ. But it goes without saying that the Mother of God, the Mother of the Lord, is an essential part of this picture. She figures in the Bible, in Luke and in John, relatively late, but with great radiance and clarity, and she has therefore always been a part of Christian life. She very quickly took on an essential significance in the Eastern

Churches, as the Council of Ephesus in 431 shows, to take just one example. And throughout history, God has never ceased to use her as the light through which he leads us to himself.

In Latin America, for instance, Mexico became Christian at the moment when our Lady appeared in Guadalupe. It was then that people realized, Yes, this is our faith, it really is here that we come to God, the Mother shows him to us, all the riches of our religions are transformed and preserved on a higher level in her. In the end, there were two figures that enabled the people of Latin America to embrace the faith: on the one hand, the Mother of God; on the other hand, the God who suffers, who also suffers in all what they themselves have experienced of violence. So we have to say that faith includes history. Cardinal Newman brought this to light. Faith develops. And part of this development is precisely the increasingly emphatic interventions by which the Mother of God enters the world as a guide along the right path, as a light from God, as the Mother through whom we are also able to know the Son and the Father in turn. God, in other words, has given us signs. In the very midst of the twentieth century. In our rationalism, and in the face of the rising power of dictatorships, God shows us the humility of the Mother, who appears to little children and speaks to them of the essentials: faith, hope, love, penance. It therefore makes sense to me that people find windows here, as it were. In Fatima I witnessed the presence of hundreds of thousands of people whose eyes, you might say, had regained the ability to see God, through all the barriers and enclosures of this world, thanks to what Mary had said to little children in Fatima.

The famous "third secret of Fatima" was not revealed until the year 2000—by Cardinal Ratzinger at the behest of John Paul II. The text speaks of a bishop clothed in white who collapses amid the bullets fired by a group of soldiers—a scene that was interpreted as a prophecy of the attempted assassination of John Paul II. Now you stated that "we would be mistaken to think that Fatima's prophetic mission is complete." What did you mean? Does the fulfillment of the message of Fatima really still lie in the future?

There are two aspects of the message of Fatima that have to be distinguished. On the one hand, there is a particular event, which is recounted in forms typical of visionary experience, and, on the other hand, there is the fundamental significance of the event. I mean, the point was not to satisfy some curiosity. If that had been the case, it would have been logical for us to publish the text much sooner. No, the purpose was to allude to a critical point, a critical moment in history, by which I mean the whole power of evil that came to a head in the major dictatorships of this twentieth century—and that in another way is still at work today.

On the other hand, the answer to this challenge is also an important point here. This answer does not consist in great political actions, but, when all is said and done, it can only come from the transformation of the heart—through faith, hope, love, and penance. In this sense, the message is precisely not a thing of the past, even though the two major dictatorships have disappeared. The Church continues to suffer, and a threat still hangs over man, so the quest for the answer continues as well, which also means that the indication Mary has given us retains its validity. Even now there is tribulation. Even now, in every conceivable form, power threatens to trample down faith. Even now, then, there is need for the answer about which the Mother of God spoke to the children.

The homily you delivered on May 13, 2010, in Fatima struck a rather dramatic note. "Mankind has succeeded in unleashing a cycle of death and terror", you proclaimed, "but failed in bringing it to an end." On that day, before half a million of the faithful, you expressed a wish that is actually quite spectacular: "May the seven years which separate us from the centenary of the apparitions", you said, "hasten the fulfillment of the prophecy of the triumph of the Immaculate Heart of Mary, to the glory of the Most Holy Trinity."

Do these words mean that the Pope, who, after all, is the holder of a prophetic office, thinks that within the coming seven years the Mother of God could actually appear in a manner that would be tantamount to a triumph?

I said that the "triumph" will draw closer. This is equivalent in meaning to our praying for the coming of God's Kingdom. This statement was not intended—I may be too rationalistic for that—to express any expectation on my part that there is going to be a huge turnaround and that history will suddenly take a totally different course. The point was rather that the power of evil is restrained again and again, that again and again the power of God himself is shown in the Mother's power and keeps it alive.

The Church is always called upon to do what God asked of Abraham, which is to see to it that there are enough righteous men to repress evil and destruction. I understood my words as a prayer that the energies of the good might regain their vigor. So you could say the triumphs of God, the triumphs of Mary, are quiet, but they are real nonetheless.

17. The Return of Jesus Christ

The German philosopher Robert Spaemann was once asked whether an internationally renowned scholar such as himself could actually believe that Jesus was born of a Virgin and worked miracles, that he rose from the dead and bestows eternal life on believers. That's just the sort of thing children believe in, isn't it? Here is how Spaemann, now eighty-three years old, answered the question: "If you want to put it like that, yes, of course. I believe roughly the same thing I believed as a child—the point is just that since then I have had more opportunity to think about my faith. In the end, thinking about my faith has always strengthened it."

What about the Pope? Does he still believe what he believed as a child?

I would answer in similar terms. I would say: Simplicity is truth—and truth is simple. Our problem is that we no longer see the forest for the trees; that for all our knowledge, we have lost the path to wisdom. This is also the idea behind Saint-Exupéry's *The Little Prince*, which shows how the cleverness of our age causes us, ironically, to overlook the essential, while the Little Prince, who hasn't the faintest idea about all this cleverness, ultimately sees more and better.

What really counts? What is authentic? What keeps us going? The key thing is to see what is simple. Why shouldn't God be capable of letting a virgin give birth, too? Why shouldn't Christ be able to rise from the dead? Of course, when I myself determine what is allowed to exist and what isn't, when *I* define the boundaries of possibility, and no one else, then of course phenomena like these have to be excluded. It is an act of intellectual arrogance for us to declare that they are internally contradictory or absurd and, for that reason alone, impossible. But it is not our business to decide how many possibilities are latent in the cosmos, how many possibilities are hidden above and in it. The message of Christ and the Church puts credible knowledge about God within our reach. God wanted to enter into this world. God didn't want us to have only a distant inkling of him through physics and mathematics. He wanted to show himself to us. And so he was able to do what the Gospels recount that he did, just as he was also able to create a new dimension of existence in the Resurrection. He was able to go beyond what Teilhard de Chardin called the biosphere and the noosphere and to institute precisely a new sphere, in which man and the world attain union with God.

Nuclear physicist Werner Heisenberg admitted that reality is designed in such a way that even the improbable is essentially possible. The Nobel Prize winner's conclusion: "The first swallow from the cup of the natural sciences makes atheists—but at the bottom of the cup God is waiting."

I would agree completely with Heisenberg there. It is only so long as one is intoxicated by individual discoveries that one says: There can't be anything more than this, now we know everything. But as soon as one recognizes the incomparable grandeur of the whole, one's vision penetrates farther and the question arises about a God who is at the origin of all things.

One of the outstanding events of your pontificate thus far has been the appearance of the first volume of your book on Jesus of Nazareth, *which is soon to be followed by the second volume. Your book marks the first time that a reigning Pope has published a decidedly theological study of Jesus Christ. Yet on the book's cover the author's name appears as Joseph Ratzinger.*

It is precisely not a book of the Magisterium, it is not a book that I wrote with my authority as Pope. Rather, it is a book that I had long planned as my last major work and that I had already begun writing before my election to the papacy. I very intentionally wanted the book to be, not an act of the Magisterium, but an effort to participate in the scholarly discussion and an attempt to propose a form of exegesis, an interpretation of Scripture, that is not beholden to a positivist historicism but that also includes faith as an element of interpretation. It is obviously a huge risk to do this, given the contemporary exegetical landscape. But it has to be done if scriptural exegesis is really serious about being theology. And if faith is meant to aid our understanding, then it must be thought of, not as hindering our access to the texts, but as facilitating it. After all, the texts emerge from faith and are designed to lead us to it.

A Pope is not elected to write bestsellers. But don't you find it nothing less than providential that you are now able to publish this book precisely at a time in your life when, after the small chair of the university, you are now the holder of the Chair of Peter, which affords you the biggest stage in the world?

I will leave that in the Lord's hands. I wanted to give people the book as a way of helping them. If it can help even more people thanks to my election to the papacy, then of course I am happy about that.

Jesus of Nazareth is the quintessential statement of a man who has spent his whole life, as priest, theologian, bishop, cardinal, and, finally, Pope, studying the figure of Jesus. What is the point that was especially important to you?

The very fact that in this man Jesus—don't forget, he is a real human being—more than a man is present. And the fact that the divine aspect wasn't tacked on to him later, as it were, in the course of successive layers of mythologization. No, already in the original figure of Jesus, in the first encounter and tradition, a reality appears that breaks through all expectations. As I have put it on other occasions, the special event stands at the *beginning*; the disciples have to receive it gradually. The Cross is at the beginning as well. At first, the disciples still try to make sense of the event in terms of generally available categories. The full stature of Jesus dawns on them only gradually, and they see with increasing clarity what was in the beginning; in other words, they see the originality of the figure of Jesus to which we refer in the *Credo* when we say "Jesus Christ, the Only Begotten Son of God, conceived by the Holy Spirit".

What does Jesus want from us?

He wants us to believe him. To let ourselves be led by him. To live with him. And so to become more and more like him and, thus, to live rightly.

Your work is an event in that it marks a paradigm shift, a turn to a new way of thinking about and handling the Gospels. The historical-critical method had its merits, but it also led fatefully

to an erroneous development. Its attempt to "demythologize"
the Bible produced a terrible superficiality and a blindness toward
the deeper layers and profound message of Scripture. What is
more, looking back, we realize that the alleged facts cited for the
last two hundred years by the skeptics intent on relativizing
pretty much every statement of the Bible were in many cases
nothing more than mere hypotheses.

Shouldn't we be much clearer than we have been that the
exegetes have to some extent been practicing a pseudo-sci-
ence whose operative principle is not Christian, but an anti-
Christian animus, and that it has led millions of people astray?

I wouldn't subscribe to quite so harsh a judgment. The
application of the historical method to the Bible as a historical text was a path that had to be taken. If we believe
that Christ is real history, and not myth, then the testimony concerning him has to be historically accessible as
well. In this sense, the historical method has also given
us many gifts. It has brought us back closer to the text
and its originality, it has shown us more precisely how it
grew, and much more besides. The historical-critical
method will always remain one dimension of interpretation. Vatican II made this clear. On the one hand, it
presents the essential elements of the historical method
as a necessary part of access to the Bible. At the same
time, though, it adds that the Bible has to be read in the
same Spirit in which it was written. It has to be read in
its wholeness, in its unity. And that can be done only
when we approach it as a book of the People of God
progressively advancing toward Christ. What is needed
is not simply a break with the historical method, but a
self-critique of the historical method; a self-critique of
historical reason that takes cognizance of its limits and

recognizes the compatibility of a type of knowledge that derives from faith; in short, we need a synthesis between an exegesis that operates with historical reason and an exegesis that is guided by faith. We have to bring the two things into a proper relationship to each other. That is also a requirement of the basic relationship between faith and reason.

One thing is clear: The evidence concerning Jesus is not limited to the Gospels but can also be gathered from a wide variety of extrabiblical sources as well. These sources rule out any doubt concerning either Jesus' historical existence or the fact that he was revered as the long-awaited Messiah. The authors of the Gospels worked on the basis of exact research, and they recorded their findings in a stirring, authentic manner, without succumbing to the temptation to smooth over or glorify. The details of their accounts agree with the historical realities.

To make things clear for the record: There is no longer any doubt, is there, that the historical Jesus and the so-called "Jesus of faith" are absolutely identical personages?

What you might call the high point of my book was the demonstration that the Jesus in whom we believe is really also the historical Jesus and that his figure, as portrayed in the Gospels, is much more realistic and credible than the numerous alternative portraits of Jesus that are paraded before us in constant succession. These alternatives are not only fleshless and bloodless, they are also unrealistic, because they make it impossible to explain how within such a short time something could suddenly appear that completely transcends ordinary expectations. Of course, your remarks threaten to stir up a whole hornets' nest of historical problems. I would put things more cautiously and say that research on points of detail remains important and useful, even though the excess of hypotheses eventually leads to absurdity. It is clear that the Gospels also reflect the concrete situation of the transmitters of the tradition and that they are clothed directly in the flesh in faith. But we cannot enter into these kinds of details here. The important point is this: The only real, historical personage is the Christ in whom the Gospels believe, and not the figure who has been reconstituted from numerous exegetical studies.

Contrary to a long-held scholarly consensus, the Gospels were written down, not at a considerable distance from the events, but quite soon after they took place. In addition, the texts have been transmitted with unprecedented fidelity to the originals. The analysis of the text historian Ulrich Victor concludes that a contemporary reader of the New Testament reads exactly the same text that was written down two thousand years ago, with the exception of a few uncertainties regarding translations of single words and certain stylistic issues.

Does this mean that the "formation" and so "transformation" of Jesus' message by the primitive community or by later generations of Christians never actually occurred, contrary to what many biblical exegetes assert?

First of all, it is clear that the texts are close in time to the events. We have direct access to the events, especially through Paul. His witness concerning the Lord's Supper and the Resurrection—1 Corinthians 11 and 15—originate literally from the 30s of the first century. Second, it is also clear and evident that the texts were treated with reverence as sacred writings and that they were put into settled form and transmitted as such first in memory and then in writing. But of course it is also correct—as we see when we compare the Synoptic Gospels—that the three Evangelists, Matthew, Mark, and Luke, transmit the very same thing with slight variations and that they arrange the chronologies and the events differently. This means that the people who handed down the traditions did relate them to the understanding of the respective communities, even as this relation brings to light the enduring elements of the past events. For this reason, we have to keep in mind that the Evangelists were not taking down minutes, records that were supposed to be mere photographs, as it were. They were practicing painstaking fidelity, but it was a fidelity that played a role in the formation process in the context of lived participation, though without influencing the essentials.

The theologian Joseph Ratzinger demonstrates with compelling facts and compelling logic that Jesus is the holder of all authority, the Lord of the universe, God himself become man. The appearance of Jesus changed the world as it had never been changed before. It was the greatest turning point and revolution in the history of mankind. And yet a residue of doubt will always remain. Could one reason be that God's Incarnation as a man simply transcends our powers of comprehension?

Yes, that's absolutely right. The point is simply that space is left for man's freedom to decide and to say Yes. God does not force himself on us. Not in the way that I can't help noticing, say, a glass on the table here, where I have no choice but to say "there it is!" His existence is an encounter that reaches down into man's inmost depths but that can never be reduced to the tangibility of a merely material thing. Consequently, the very magnitude of the reality is such that faith is always an event that happens in freedom. This event contains the certainty that there is something true, something real here—but, on the other hand, it never completely excludes the possibility of denial.

Doesn't the study of Christ's life and teaching always have to be a question for the Church as well? Isn't it the case, especially when as an author you take a fresh look at these topics, that you inevitably start reeling when you realize how far the Church has repeatedly strayed from the path that the Son of God showed her?

Well, right now, in the midst of the scandals, we have experienced what it means to be very stunned by how wretched the Church is, by how much her members fail to follow Christ. That is the one side, which we are forced to experience for our humiliation, for our real humility. The other side is that, in spite of everything, he does not release his grip on the Church. In spite of the weakness of the people in whom he shows himself, he keeps the Church in his grasp, he raises up saints in her, and makes himself present through them. I believe that these two feelings belong together: the deep shock over the wretchedness, the sinfulness of the Church—and the deep shock over the fact that he doesn't drop this instrument, but that he works with it; that he never ceases to show himself through and in the Church.

Jesus does not merely bring a message, he is also the Savior, the healer, Christus medicus, *as an old expression has it. Given this society of ours, which is so broken and unhealthy in so many ways, as we have often said in this interview, isn't it an especially pressing task of the Church to take extra pains to highlight the offer of salvation contained in the Gospel? Jesus, at any rate, made his disciples strong enough, not just to preach, but also to expel demons and to heal.*

Yes, that's key. The Church is not here to place burdens on the shoulders of mankind, and she does not offer some sort of moral system. The really crucial thing is that the Church offers Him. That she opens wide the doors to God and so gives people what they are most waiting for and what can most help them. The Church does this mainly through the great miracle of love, which never stops happening afresh. When people—without earning any profit, without having to do it because it is their job—are motivated by Christ to stand by others and to help them. You are right that this therapeutic character of Christianity, as Eugen Biser put it, ought to be much more clearly in evidence than it is.

A major problem for Christians is that they stand unprotected in the middle of a world that is basically continually launching bombs against the alternative values of Christian culture. Wouldn't you have to say that it is impossible to be entirely immune to this sort of worldwide propaganda in favor of negative behavior?

It is true that we need something like islands where faith in God and the interior simplicity of Christianity are alive and radiant; oases, Noah's arks, to which man can always come back for refuge. Liturgical spaces offer such protective zones. But there are also various communities and movements, the parishes, celebrations of the sacraments, exercises of piety, pilgrimages, and so forth, in which the Church attempts to instill powers of resistance as well as to develop protective zones in which the beauty of the world, of the gift of being alive, also becomes visible in contrast to the rampant brokenness around us.

18. On the Last Things

Jesus warned his disciples against the sword, but he didn't leave them unequipped. He promised to "send the Spirit". Does this promise have something to do with a way of thinking that transcends the mundane? Does it involve some sort of spiritual intelligence that we could rediscover afresh today?

Obviously we shouldn't picture this in too mechanical a way. It is not as if, to use an image, an extra floor were added on top of our ordinary existence. The point is rather that inward contact with God through, with, and in Christ really does open in us new possibilities and enlarge our heart and our spirit. Faith truly does give our life a further dimension.

It might be something like a meta-net, perhaps infinitely faster than the Internet, but in any case freer, truer, and more positive.

Which, when you think about it, is the idea that was expressed in the term *"communio sanctorum"*: that we are all somehow profoundly united and that we all recognize one another, even if we have never seen one another, because the same Spirit, the same Lord, is at work in us.

In your address in Lisbon, you stated that a primary task of the Church today consists in enabling people "to look beyond

*penultimate realities and to seek those that are ultimate".
The doctrine of "the last things" is a central part of the pat-
rimony of the faith. It deals with topics such as hell, purga-
tory, the Antichrist, the persecution of the Church in the end
times, Christ's Second Coming, and the Last Judgment.
Why are the preachers so deafeningly silent about eschatology,
despite the fact that eschatological issues really do affect everyone existentially, unlike many "ever-recurring topics" within
the Church?*

That is a very serious question. Our preaching, our proclamation, really is one-sided, in that it is largely directed
toward the creation of a better world, while hardly
anyone talks any more about the other, truly better
world. We need to examine our consciences on this
point. Of course one has to meet one's listeners halfway, one has to speak to them in terms of their own
horizon. But at the same time our task is to open up
this horizon, to broaden it, and to turn our gaze toward
the ultimate.

These things are hard to accept for people today and
seem unreal to them. Instead, they want concrete answers
for now, for the tribulations of everyday life. But these
answers are incomplete so long as they don't convey the
sense and the interior realization that I am more than this
material life, that there is a judgment, and that grace and
eternity exist. By the same token, we also need to find
new words and new means to enable people to break
through the sound barrier of finitude.

*All of Jesus' prophecies have come to pass, except one that has
yet to be fulfilled: the prophecy of his Second Coming. Its fulfillment will finally make the word "redemption" fully true. You*

*have coined the term "eschatological realism". What exactly does
that mean?*

It means that these things are not a fata morgana or some
kind of fictitious utopia, but that they correspond exactly
to reality. In fact, we always have to keep present in our
minds the fact that he tells us with the greatest certainty
"I will come again." This statement comes before everything else. This is also why the Mass was originally celebrated facing east, toward the returning Lord, who is
symbolized in the rising sun. Every Mass is therefore an act
of going out to meet the One who is coming. In this way,
his coming is also anticipated, as it were; we go out to meet
him—and he comes, anticipatively, already now. I like to
compare this with the account of the wedding at Cana. The
first thing the Lord says to Mary there is "My hour has not
yet come." But then, in spite of that, he gives the new wine,
as it were, anticipating his hour, which is yet to come. This
eschatological realism becomes present in the Eucharist: we
go out to meet him—as the One who comes—and he
comes already now in anticipation of this hour, which one
day will arrive once and for all. If we understand this as we
should, we will go out to meet the Lord who has already
been coming all along, we will enter into his coming—
and so will allow ourselves to be fitted into a greater reality, beyond the everyday, just as we were saying before.

*About eighty years ago, Faustina Kowalska, the Polish nun
canonized by John Paul II, heard Jesus say in a vision "You
will prepare the world for my definitive return." Are we obliged
to believe that?*

If one took this statement in a chronological sense, as an
injunction to get ready, as it were, immediately for the

Second Coming, it would be false. But it is correct if one understands it in the spiritual sense that was just explained, as meaning that the Lord is always the One who comes and that we are always also preparing ourselves for his definitive coming, precisely when we go out to meet his mercy and allow ourselves to be formed by him. By letting ourselves be formed by God's gift of mercy as a force to counteract the mercilessness of the world, then we prepare, as it were, for his own coming in person and for his mercy.

I would like to introduce another issue along the same lines. The only prophetic book of the New Testament, the "Secret Revelation of Saint John", the Book of Revelation, which is understood as a proclamation of the good news, is entirely oriented toward Christ's second appearing. Even before that, in Jesus' own time, Jewish Scripture scholars, not to mention monks and astronomers, had tried to calculate the date of the Messiah's coming.

Meanwhile, the German scholar Rüdiger Holinski claims to have discovered that the letters to the seven communities at the beginning of the Book of Revelation are not about actual places but contain coded references to the seven successive epochs of Church history. For example, the name of the seventh and last community, Laodicea (translated "the right of the people"), supposedly stands for a general popular uprising and the demand for participation. The parallel "seventh seal" would then stand for an epoch supposedly marked by anxiety, depression, false teachers in the Church, and new religions, a time in which works are neither hot nor cold.

Be that as it may, the fact is that the world is in graver danger today than in almost any previous period of its history. As we have already discussed here, the devastation of the planet on which we live has in many areas reached the point of no return. The situation of the faith is marked by dramatic changes. The sense of belief is withering, churches are forced to close, an anti-Christian dictatorship of public opinion has shed the mask of subtlety and turned to open aggression instead. On top of all of this, man has now begun to break the ultimate biblical taboo, the "tree of life", the manipulation and production of life itself. Did this state of affairs cause you to remark in Jesus of Nazareth *that we should apply especially Jesus' sayings about judgment to the present situation?*

I am skeptical about interpretations like the one you mentioned. The Book of Revelation is a mysterious text and has many dimensions. But whether the claims of this particular interpreter are part of that is a question I would leave open. In any case, Revelation provides no system for calculating at what point in time things are going to occur. In fact, the striking aspect of Revelation is precisely that it is just when one thinks the end is truly now upon us that the whole thing starts again from the beginning. In other words, Revelation presents us with a mysterious mirror in which we see that tribulations continue, but without also being told exactly when and how an answer will come or when and how the Lord will show himself to us.

We are not dealing with a book suited for calculating chronologies. The important thing is that every period open itself to the presence of the Lord. That even we, here and now, stand under the Lord's judgment and that we let ourselves be guided by his judgment. Whereas people had previously spoken only of a twofold coming of Christ—once in Bethlehem and again at the end of time—Saint Bernard of Clairvaux spoke of an *adventus medius*,

of an intermediate coming, thanks to which he period-
ically renews his intervention in history.

I believe that Bernard's distinction strikes just the right
note. We cannot pin down when the world will end.
Christ himself says that no one knows the hour, not even
the Son. But we must always stand in the imminence of
his coming, as it were—and we must be certain, especially in the midst of tribulations, that he is near. At the
same time, when we act we should be aware that we are
under judgment.

We do not know when it will be, but we know from the Gos-
pel that it will be. As we read in Matthew, "when the Son of
man comes in his glory, and all the angels with him, he will sit
on his glorious throne." He will, Matthew continues, divide
humanity like a shepherd separates the sheep from the goats. To
the ones on his right, he will say: "Inherit the kingdom pre-
pared for you from the foundation of the world." But to the
others, he will say: "Depart from me, you cursed, into the eter-
nal fire."

The unequivocal clarity of Jesus' warnings is further under-
scored in John's Gospel: "I have come as light into the world,
that whoever believes in me may not remain in darkness." There
are many other such statements about judgment as well. Are
these sayings meant only symbolically?

Of course not. A real Last Judgment takes place here.
When you think about it, this judgment is always coming upon man already in, shall we say, a penultimate form:
in his death. The grand tableau that is painted especially
in Matthew 25, with the sheep and the goats, is a parable
for a reality that is unimaginable. After all, we are dealing with an utterly unique event that we cannot picture

to ourselves; the fact that the whole cosmos now stands
before the Lord, that the whole of history stands before
him. This has to be expressed in images that convey to
us an inkling of what is going on. How it will all look
physically escapes our ability to imagine. But that he is
the judge, that a real judgment takes place, that humanity is divided, so that there is also, just as we said, a possibility of damnation, that things are not equally valid,
are all very important truths. People nowadays tend to
say, why worry, all these bad things won't really happen.
God can't really be like that in the end. No, he takes us
seriously. And there is the fact that evil continues to exist
and must be condemned. In this sense, while being joy-
fully grateful that God is so good and that he graciously
pardons us, we should perceive the seriousness of evil,
which we have seen in Nazism and Communism and
which we also see all around us today. And we should
shape our lives accordingly.

Fourteen years ago I asked you whether it is still even worth-
while to get onboard the barque of the Church, which seems
somewhat decrepit with old age. Today the question is: Isn't the
Church actually looking more like Noah's ark all the time?
What does the Pope think? Is there still any chance at all for
us to save our planet by our own power?

Man is in any case incapable of mastering history by his
own power. Man is clearly in danger, and he is endan-
gering both himself and the world; we could even say
we have scientific evidence of this. Man can be saved
only when moral energies gather strength in his heart;
energies that can come only from the encounter with
God; energies of resistance. We therefore need him, the

Other, who helps us be what we ourselves cannot be; and we need Christ, who gathers us into a communion that we call the Church.

According to the Gospel of John, Jesus says at a certain key point that what counts is the mission of the Father: "And I know that his mission is everlasting life." Is that the reason why Jesus came into the world?

Certainly. That is the important thing. That we become capable of God and so are enabled to enter into eternal life. Yes, he came so that we might come to know the truth. So that we might touch God. So that the door might be open. So that we might find life, the real life, that is no longer subject to death.

APPENDIX

Serious Sins against Defenseless Children

*From the Pastoral Letter
to the Catholics of Ireland, dated March 19, 2010*

I can only share in the dismay and the sense of betrayal that so many of you have experienced on learning of these sinful and criminal acts and the way Church authorities in Ireland dealt with them. . . .

At the same time, I must also express my conviction that, in order to recover from this grievous wound, the Church in Ireland must first acknowledge before the Lord and before others the serious sins committed against defenseless children. Such an acknowledgment, accompanied by sincere sorrow for the damage caused to these victims and their families, must lead to a concerted effort to ensure the protection of children from similar crimes in the future. . . .

Only by examining carefully the many elements that gave rise to the present crisis can a clear-sighted diagnosis of its causes be undertaken and effective remedies be found. Certainly, among the contributing factors we can include: inadequate procedures for determining the suitability of candidates for the priesthood and the religious life; insufficient human, moral, intellectual, and spiritual formation in seminaries and novitiates; a tendency in society to favor the clergy and other authority figures; and a misplaced concern for the reputation of the Church and the avoidance of scandal, resulting in failure to apply existing canonical penalties and to safeguard the dignity of every person. . . .

To the victims of abuse and their families: You have suffered grievously, and I am truly sorry. I know that nothing can undo the wrong you have endured. Your trust has been betrayed, and your dignity has been violated. Many of you found that, when you were courageous enough to speak of what happened to you, no one would listen. Those of you who were abused in residential institutions must have felt that there was no escape from your sufferings. It is understandable that you find it hard to forgive or be reconciled with the Church. In her name, I openly express the shame and remorse that we all feel....

To priests and religious who have abused children: You betrayed the trust that was placed in you by innocent young people and their parents, and you must answer for it before Almighty God and before properly constituted tribunals. You have forfeited the esteem of the people of Ireland and brought shame and dishonor upon your confreres. Those of you who are priests violated the sanctity of the sacrament of Holy Orders in which Christ makes himself present in us and in our actions. Together with the immense harm done to victims, great damage has been done to the Church and to the public perception of the priesthood and religious life.

I urge you to examine your conscience, take responsibility for the sins you have committed, and humbly express your sorrow.... Openly acknowledge your guilt, submit yourselves to the demands of justice, but do not despair of God's mercy....

To my brother bishops: It cannot be denied that some of you and your predecessors failed, at times grievously, to apply the long-established norms of canon law to the crime of child abuse. Serious mistakes were made in responding to allegations. I recognize how difficult it was to grasp the extent and complexity of the problem, to obtain reliable information, and to make the right decisions in the light of conflicting expert advice. Nevertheless, it must be admitted that grave errors of judgment were made and failures of leadership occurred. All this has seriously undermined your credibility and effectiveness.... Besides fully implementing the norms of canon law in addressing cases of child abuse, continue to cooperate with the civil authorities in their area of competence.... Only decisive action carried out with complete honesty and transparency will restore the respect and good will of the Irish people towards the Church to which we have consecrated our lives....

(Translation taken from
the Vatican website.)

Faith and Violence

*From the "Regensburg Address",
dated September 12, 2006*

Without descending to details, such as the difference in treatment accorded to those who have the "Book" and the "infidels", [the Byzantine emperor, Manuel II Paleologus] addresses his interlocutor with a startling brusqueness, a brusqueness that we find unacceptable, on the central question about the relationship between religion and violence in general, saying: "Show me just what Mohammed brought that was new, and there you will find things only evil and inhuman, such as his command to spread by the sword the faith he preached." The emperor, after having expressed himself so forcefully, goes on to explain in detail the reasons why spreading the faith through violence is something unreasonable. Violence is incompatible with the nature of God and the nature of the soul. "God", he says, "is not pleased by blood—and not acting reasonably (σὺν λόγω) is contrary to God's nature. Faith is born of the soul, not the body. Whoever would lead someone to faith needs the ability to speak well and to reason properly, without violence and threats...."

(Translation taken from
the Vatican website.)

AIDS and the Humanization of Sexuality

*From the Interview during the Flight to Cameroon
on March 17, 2009*

Father Lombardi: Now a further question from a French
speaker: our colleague Philippe Visseyrias from France 2:

*Question: Your Holiness, among the many ills that beset Africa,
one of the most pressing is the spread of AIDS. The position of
the Catholic Church on the way to fight it is often considered
unrealistic and ineffective. Will you address this theme during
the journey? Holy Father, would you be able to respond in
French to this question?*

Benedict XVI: I would say the opposite. I think that the
most efficient, most truly present player in the fight against
AIDS is the Catholic Church herself, with her movements and her various organizations. I think of the
Sant'Egidio community that does so much, visibly and also
behind the scenes, in the struggle against AIDS, I think
of the Camillians, and so much more besides, I think of
all the Sisters who take care of the sick.... I would say
that this problem of AIDS cannot be overcome merely
with money, necessary though it is. If there is no human
dimension, if Africans do not help [*by responsible behavior*], the problem cannot be overcome by the distribution
of prophylactics: on the contrary, they increase it.

The solution must have two elements: firstly, bringing
out the human dimension of sexuality, that is to say a
spiritual and human renewal that would bring with it a
new way of behaving towards others, and secondly, true

friendship offered above all to those who are suffering, a willingness to make sacrifices and to practice self-denial, to be alongside the suffering. And so these are the factors that help and that lead to real progress: our twofold effort to renew humanity inwardly, to give spiritual and human strength for proper conduct towards our bodies and those of others, and this capacity to suffer with those who are suffering, to remain present in situations of trial. It seems to me that this is the proper response, and the Church does this, thereby offering an enormous and important contribution. We thank all who do so.

(Translation taken from
the Vatican website.)

Benedict XVI
Curriculum Vitae and a Brief Chronicle of the Pontificate

Biography until his Election as Pope

1927–1937

Born Joseph Alois Ratzinger on Holy Saturday, April 16, 1927, at 4:15 A.M. in Marktl am Inn, in the rural district of Altötting. His parents are the police chief Joseph Ratzinger (b. March 6, 1877; d. August 25, 1959) and Maria Ratzinger (b. January 8, 1884; d. December 16, 1963), a baker's daughter. Joseph is the third and last child of the couple, after Maria Theogona (b. December 7, 1921; d. November 2, 1991) and Georg (b. January 15, 1924). In July 1929, the family moves to Tittmoning; in December 1932, to Aschau am Inn, where he starts school. From 1937 on, the family lives in Hufschlag bei Traunstein.

1937–1945

1937: Admitted to the *Gymnasium* [secondary school] in Traunstein. 1939: Enters St. Michael Seminary, the archdiocesan minor seminary in Traunstein. 1943–1945: War service as assistant in anti-aircraft defense, in work service, and as an infantry soldier; May–June 1945: Imprisonment at American P.O.W. camp in Neu-Ulm. 1945: Graduates from Chiemgau Gymnasium in Traunstein.

1945–1951

December 1945–Summer 1947: Studies philosophy at the College [*Hochschule*] for Philosophy and Theology in Freising near Munich, followed by studies in theology at the University of Munich. Late autumn 1950–June 1951: Postgraduate work in Freising while preparing for priestly ordination.

1951–1953

Ordained a priest on June 29, 1951, in Freising together with his brother Georg by Michael Cardinal Faulhaber. July 1951: Assistant priest in Munich-Moosach (St. Martin parish). From August 1, 1951, on: Chaplain in Munich-Bogenhausen (Precious Blood parish). October 1952 to summer 1954: Instructor at the major seminary in Freising while assisting at the churches in Freising. July 1953: Doctorate in theology at the University of Munich (Dissertation: "People and House of God in St. Augustine's Doctrine of the Church").

1954–1959

As of the winter semester 1954/1955: Instructor for dogmatic and fundamental theology at the College of Philosophy and Theology in Freising. 1957: Completed *Habilitation* [post-doctoral dissertation] at the University of Munich in the department of fundamental theology on the topic of "The Theology of History in St. Bonaventure". 1958–1959: Extraordinary professor for dogmatic and fundamental theology in Freising.

1959–1963

Ordinary professor for fundamental theology at the University of Bonn. Theme of his inaugural lecture: "The God of Faith and the God of the Philosophers".

1962–1965

Advisor to Cardinal Joseph Frings of Cologne and official conciliar theologian (*peritus*) at Vatican II. Member of the Doctrinal Committee of the German Bishops and of the International Pontifical Theological Commission in Rome.

1963–1966

Ordinary professor for dogmatics and the history of dogma at the University of Münster (Inaugural lecture: "Revelation and Tradition").

1966–1969

Ordinary professor for dogmatics and the history of dogma at the University of Tübingen. In 1968 his book *Introduction to Christianity* is published.

1969–1977

Ordinary professor for dogmatics and the history of dogma at the University of Regensburg. In 1972, together with Hans Urs von Balthasar, Henri de Lubac, and others, founds the International Catholic Journal *Communio*; 1976/1977: Vice President of the University of Regensburg.

1977–1982

March 25, 1977: Appointed Archbishop of Munich and Freising by Pope Paul VI, consecrated bishop on May 28. His episcopal motto is: *"Cooperatores veritatis"* (Co-workers of the truth) (cf. 3 John 8). June 27, 1977: Created cardinal. Engaged as honorary professor at the University of Regensburg.

1978: The year of the three Popes. After the death of Paul VI (August 6), participates in the conclave that elects Albino Luciani as Pope John Paul I; after Luciani's death (September 28), participates in the conclave from which, on October 16, Cardinal Karol Wojtyła, Archbishop of Krakow, emerges as Pope John Paul II; Ratzinger decisively supported his election. Wojtyła is the first non-Italian on the Chair of Peter since 1523.

1981–2005

November 25, 1981: Appointed Prefect of the Congregation for the Doctrine of the Faith (CDF) and thereby also President of the Pontifical Biblical Commission and the International Theological Commission by Pope John Paul II. (Departure from Munich and commencement of these duties in March 1982).

1986–1992: Head of the Pontifical Commission for the preparation of the *Catechism of the Catholic Church* (which is presented on December 12, 1992). 1991: Member of the European Academy of Arts and Sciences. 1992: Elected member of the *Académie des sciences morales et politiques* of the *Institut de France*, Paris. 1993: Promoted to Cardinal-Archbishop of the suburbicarian Diocese of Velletri-Segni. 1998: Opening of the Archives of the former Office of the Inquisition at Ratzinger's request; elected Vice Dean of the College of Cardinals; appointed Commander of the Legion of Honor by the President of France.

1999: Ratzinger signs the "Joint Declaration on the Doctrine of Justification" by the Catholic Church and the Lutheran World Federation, an ecumenical achievement in which he played a leading role. 2000: Publication of the Declaration *Dominus Iesus* "On the Unicity and Salvific Universality of Jesus Christ and the Church"; as of November 13, 2000, Honorary Member of the Pontifical Academy of Sciences. 2001: In view of numerous instances of child abuse by clerics and the inadequate response to them by ecclesiastical authorities, Ratzinger transfers jurisdiction over such cases to the CDF and begins to process 3,000 cases; new procedures are established in the Vatican (2001) and in Germany (2002). 2002: Elected Dean of the College of Cardinals with the suburbicarian See of Ostia; participates in the World Day of Prayer in Assisi.

Further duties in the Roman Curia during this time: Member of the Council of the Secretary of State for Relations with States and of the following Congregations: for the Oriental Churches, for Divine Worship and the Discipline of the Sacraments, for Bishops, for the Evangelization of Peoples, for Catholic Education, for the Clergy, and for the Causes of Saints; member of the following Pontifical Councils: for Promoting Christian Unity, for Culture; member of the Supreme Tribunal of the Apostolic Signatura; member of the following Pontifical Commissions: for Latin America, *Ecclesia Dei*, for the Interpretation of Legislative Texts, for the Revision of the Code of Oriental Canon Law.

Honorary doctorates: College of St. Thomas in St. Paul, Minnesota (1984), Catholic University of Lima (1986),

Catholic University of Eichstätt (1987), Catholic University of Lublin (1988), University of Navarra in Pamplona (1998), Free University "Maria Santissima Assunta (LUMSA)" in Rome (1999), University of Breslau (2000).

Brief Chronicle of the Pontificate

2005

April 2. Death of John Paul II.

April 8. As Dean of the College of Cardinals, Cardinal Ratzinger presides at the funeral ceremonies for the deceased Pope and also at the following conclave. The Funeral Mass for John Paul II, attended by as many as five million, is presumably the largest religious event in the history of mankind.

April 18. Beginning of the conclave with the entrance of the 115 cardinals eligible to vote into the Sistine Chapel; Ratzinger's opening address on "relativism".

April 19. From an especially short, 26-hour conclave, Joseph Ratzinger emerges as the 265th Pope in the history of the Roman Catholic Church. The new Pontiff takes the name *Benedict*, recalling the monastic founder Benedict of Nursia, but also his predecessor Benedict XV, who because of his peace initiatives during World War I was described as the "Pope of peace".

Benedict XVI is the first Pope in the modern era to design his coat of arms without the tiara (which among other things is a symbol of the secular power of the Church), replacing it with a simple bishop's miter. On the other hand, for the first time a pallium (stole worn by metropolitan bishops) is included in a papal coat of arms.

April 24. Inaugural Mass on St. Peter's Square, with 500,000 pilgrims and dignitaries in attendance. Benedict wears the pallium in the Orthodox style—an expression of sympathy and a reference to the period before the Eastern Schism of 1054, when the Church of the East and of the West was still united under the successors of Peter.

May 29. Pastoral visit to Bari at the conclusion of the Italian National Eucharistic Congress. Benedict XVI emphasizes the central importance of Sunday and the Eucharist: "Without Sunday we cannot live."

June 9. Meeting with representatives of the International Jewish Committee for Interreligious Consultations.[1]

June 16. Meeting with the General Secretary of the World Council of Churches, Rev. Dr. Samuel Kobia.

June 24. State visit with Italian President Carlo Ciampi in the Quirinal Palace in Rome. The visit had been planned by John Paul II and was meant to foster rapprochement between the Vatican and the Italian State after twenty years of estrangement.

---

[1] Week after week the Pope receives numerous presidents and government officials. In the interests of brevity, only a few special meetings will be listed in this chronicle. Therefore it is not possible to mention a large number of meetings with priests, theologians, bishops making their *ad limina* visits, accreditations of diplomats, beatifications and canonizations, addresses, messages, letters, liturgical celebrations, appointments, visits to the sick, etc.

June 28. Motu proprio approving and publishing the *Compendium of the Catechism of the Catholic Church.*[2]

June 30. Meeting with the delegation of the Ecumenical Patriarch Bartholomew I on the occasion of the beginning of the new pontificate.

August 18–21. Apostolic visit to Cologne, Germany, on the occasion of the 20th World Youth Day. *August 19*: Visit to the synagogue in Cologne. This is the first papal visit to a Jewish house of prayer in Germany. *August 21*: Concluding Mass for World Youth Day in Cologne with over a million young people.

September 20. Benedict XVI grants a television interview— the first ever for a Pope—to the Polish network TVP.

September 24. Four-hour discussion with Hans Küng, a theologian from Tübingen and critic of the Church, whose faculties to teach Catholic theology were withdrawn in 1979 by John Paul II.

October 2–23. Regular General Assembly of the 11th World Synod of Bishops on the theme, "The Eucharist: Source and Summit of the Church's Life and Mission". For the first time a Pope takes part in the discussion at a Synod of Bishops. Furthermore, Benedict introduces free debate, so as to discuss controversies in "salutary commotion".

November 7. Meeting with the President of the Lutheran World Federation, Bishop Mark Hanson.

---

[2]All papal documents, whether apostolic letters or encyclicals, are listed according to the date on which they were signed, not when they were published.

November 17. Meeting with Israeli President Moshe Katzav, who invites Pope Benedict to visit the Holy Land.

December 3. Meeting with the Palestinian leader Mahmoud Abbas, who voices an invitation to visit Palestine.

December 25. First encyclical, *Deus caritas est* (God Is Love), in which Pope Benedict describes love as the central dimension of Christianity.

2006

February 18. Publication of the *Annuario Pontificio* [Pontifical Yearbook] 2006, in which for the first time the honorific title "Patriarch of the West" no longer appears among the official titles of the Pope. The omission of the title is an ecumenical gesture vis-à-vis the Orthodox Churches.

March 11. Reform of the Curia by merging the leadership of the "Pontifical Council for Pastoral Care of Migrants and Itinerant Peoples" and the "Pontifical Council for Justice and Peace", and also by merging the leadership of the "Pontifical Council for Interreligious Dialogue" and the "Pontifical Council for Culture".

May 20. Meeting with Russian Orthodox Metropolitan Kirill.

May 25–28. Apostolic visit to Poland. *May 26*: Visit to the Shrine of Jasna Gorá in Czestochowa. *May 27*: Visit to the birthplace of John Paul II in Wadowice; meeting with 60,000 young people in Krakow. *May 28*: Mass attended by 1.2 million people in Krakow; visit to the Auschwitz-Birkenau concentration camp. This stop on the itinerary was not planned at first. Benedict, however, insisted on this visit. "It was impossible for me not to come here as Pope."

June 3. Celebration of Mass with 350,000 members of ecclesial movements and new communities on St. Peter's Square.

July 8–9. Apostolic visit to Valencia, Spain. The occasion is the Fifth World Family Congress. "The family is a necessary good for peoples, an indispensable foundation for society and a great and lifelong treasure for couples" (Address on July 8).

September 1. Pilgrimage to the Shrine of the "Holy Face" of Manoppello, Italy.

September 9–14. Apostolic visit to Bavaria, with stops in Munich, Altötting, Marktl (the Pope's birthplace), Regensburg, and Freising. *September 12*: Academic lecture at the University of Regensburg. In it Benedict cites a statement by the late medieval Byzantine Emperor Manuel II Paleologus concerning the role of violence in Islam, which leads to organized Muslim protests worldwide, in which churches are desecrated and a nun loses her life.

September 15. After the resignation of Angelo Sodano upon reaching the age of retirement, the appointment of Tarcisio Bertone as the new Cardinal Secretary of State.

October 19. Visit to Verona on the occasion of the Fourth National Congress of the Italian Church.

November 28–December 1. Apostolic visit to Turkey. *November 28*: Meeting with the Turkish Prime Minister Recep Tayyip Erdoğan. *November 29*: Meeting with the

Ecumenical Patriarch Bartholomew I, the honorary primate of all Orthodox Christians. *November 30*: Celebration of the Feast of St. Andrew together with Patriarch Bartholomew and signing of a joint declaration on the rapprochement of Catholics and Orthodox; meeting with the Armenian Patriarch Mesrob II Mutafyan; visit to the Sultan Ahmed Mosque in Istanbul—the second papal visit ever to an Islamic house of prayer.

December 13. Meeting with the Israeli Prime Minister Ehud Olmert for a discussion about the situation in the Near East and in Lebanon.

December 15. Meeting with the Coptic Patriarch Antonios Naguib.

December 16. Letter to German Federal Chancellor Angela Merkel before the G-8 Summit Meeting in Heiligendamm, in which the Pope calls for debt forgiveness for the poorest nations.

2007

January 25. Meeting with the Prime Minister of Vietnam, Nguyen Tan Dung. This is the first visit of a Vietnamese head of government to the Vatican since the Communist seizure of power in 1975.

February 22. Post-synodal apostolic exhortation *Sacramentum Caritatis* on the Eucharist as the source and summit of the Church's life and mission.

March 13. Meeting with Russian President Vladimir Putin. The discussion focuses on the relations between the

Catholic Church and the Russian Orthodox Church and on the situation in the Near East.

March 20. Meeting with the General Secretary of the United Nations, Ban Ki-Moon.

March 24. Meeting with 80,000 members and associates of the ecclesial movement *Communione e Liberazione* on St. Peter's Square.

April 16. Publication of volume 1 of the book *Jesus of Nazareth* on the Pope's 80th birthday.

April 21–22. Pastoral visit to Vigevano in the Lombardy region, the only Italian diocese that John Paul II did not visit during his almost 27 years in office, and Pavia, where Pope Benedict makes a pilgrimage to the tomb of St. Augustine.

May 4. Meeting with the Chairman of the German Bishops' Conference, Bishop Wolfgang Huber.

May 9–14. Apostolic visit to Brazil. *May 9:* Benedict XVI calls Latin America "the Continent of Hope". *May 10.* Meeting with President Luiz Inácio Lula da Silva in São Paulo. *May 12:* At his own request, the Pope visits the *Fazenda da Esperança*, a rehabilitation project especially for drug-addicted youth. *May 13:* Opening of the Fifth General Conference of the Episcopate of Latin America and the Caribbean in Aparecida.

May 23. In his general audience, the Pope speaks about his trip to Latin America and also mentions "unjustifiable crimes" during the colonization and Christianization of the continent.

May 27. Letter to the Catholics of China, in which Pope Benedict calls upon the 12 million faithful, who are split into two camps, to join together under his leadership and calls upon the government in Beijing to resume diplomatic relationships with the Vatican.

June 9. U.S. President George W. Bush speaks with Pope Benedict XVI about the situation in the Near and Middle East.

June 11. Motu proprio *De aliquibus mutationibus in normis de electione Romani Pontificis* about several changes in the norms concerning a papal election. It states that in a conclave a two-thirds majority is required, even after the 33rd ballot. (Previously a simple majority was then sufficient.)

June 17. Pastoral visit to Assisi on the occasion of the 800th anniversary of the conversion of St. Francis.

June 21. Meeting with the Assyrian Patriarch Mar Dinkha IV.

June 25. Separation of the administration of the Pontifical Council for Interreligious Dialogue from that of the Pontifical Council for Culture.

July 7. Motu proprio *Summorum Pontificum* on the Roman liturgy according to the liturgical books prior to the reform carried out in 1970. Accordingly, besides the ordinary form of the Roman Rite, it is also permitted to celebrate now with a congregation, as the extraordinary form, the so-called "Tridentine Mass" that was in force until the Council; this no longer requires permission from the competent bishop, as was previously the case.

September 1–2. Pastoral visit to Loreto on the occasion of the *Agora*, a meeting with several hundred thousand Italian youth, as a national preparation for World Youth Day in Sydney.

September 6. Meeting with Israeli Prime Minister Shimon Peres.

September 7–9. Apostolic visit to Austria. The occasion of the 850th anniversary of the founding of the pilgrimage shrine Mariazell. In Vienna the Pope speaks once more about the culture of Sunday.

September 23. Pastoral visit to Velletri, Italy, where Joseph Ratzinger was titular bishop for 12 years before his election to the papacy.

October 8. Meeting with the leader of the World Jewish Congress, Ronald Lauder.

October 19. First official meeting in history of a Pope with representatives of the Mennonites.

October 21. Pastoral visit in Naples. The occasion is the 21st International Peace Conference. Among the participants are the Ecumenical Patriarch of Constantinople, Bartholomew I, the Anglican Archbishop of Canterbury, Rowan Williams, the Chairman of the German Bishops' Conference, Wolfgang Huber, the Israeli Chief Rabbi Yona Metzger, and the Rector of Al-Azhar University in Egypt, Ahmad Al-Tayyeb.

November 6. Meeting with the Saudi-Arabian King Abdullah, protector of the holy places of Islam. It is the first audience of a Saudi monarch with the leader of the Catholic Church.

November 30. Second encyclical, *Spe salvi* (Saved in Hope) on Christian hope even beyond death.

December 6. Meeting with representatives of the Baptist World Alliance.

December 7. Meeting with the leader of the Foreign Office of the Russian Orthodox Church, Metropolitan Kirill, later called to be the Patriarch of his Church.

2008

February 5. Change of the Good Friday intercession "for the Jews" within the Tridentine Mass to a theologically adapted wording.

March 6. Meeting with the Ecumenical Patriarch of Constantinople, Bartholomew I.

April 15–21. Apostolic visit to the United States of America and the United Nations. *April 16*: Meeting with U.S. President George W. Bush in the White House. *April 17*: For the first time a Pope meets with men and women who have been sexually abused by Catholic priests; publication of the April 14 message to the worldwide Jewish community on the Feast of Passover. *April 18*: Address to the General Assembly of the United Nations in New York. Respect for human rights is a central theme; visit to the Park East Synagogue in Manhattan. *April 20*: Prayer for the victims of the terrorist attacks on September 11, 2001, at Ground Zero.

April 16. Message of the Pope on Russian television.

May 2. Meeting with a delegation of Shiite Muslims from Iran. The Holy See and Iranian theologians had previously agreed on a joint declaration on the topic of "Faith and Reason in Christianity and in Islam". According to the document there is agreement that faith and reason "are intrinsically non-violent" and should never be used for acts of violence.

May 5. Meeting with the Primate of the Anglicans, Archbishop Rowan Williams of Canterbury.

May 8. Meeting with the Greek-Melkite Patriarch of Antioch, Gregorios III Laham.

May 9. Ecumenical celebration with the Supreme Patriarch and Katholikos of all Armenians, Karekin II.

May 17–18. Pastoral visit in Savona and Genoa.

June 13. Meeting with U.S. President George W. Bush.

June 14–15. Pastoral visit in Santa Maria di Leuca and Brindisi.

June 21. Apostolic letter *Antiqua ordinatione*. The motu proprio concerns the judicial structure of the Apostolic Signatura. It was published exclusively in Latin.

June 28–29. Inauguration of the Year of St. Paul together with the Ecumenical Patriarch Bartholomew I.

July 12–21. Apostolic visit to Sydney. The occasion is the 23rd World Youth Day. *July 17*: Meeting with representatives of the Australian government. *July 19*: Holy Mass in St. Mary's Cathedral in Sydney, in which Pope Benedict asks for forgiveness for the sexual abuse of children by Catholic clergy and religious in Australia. He acknowledges "the shame which we have all felt as a result of the sexual abuse of minors by some clergy and religious in this country. Indeed, I am deeply sorry for the pain and suffering the victims have endured, and I assure them that, as their Pastor, I too share in their suffering." *July 20*: Concluding Mass in Sydney. With around 500,00 in attendance, Pope Benedict XVI calls for a renewal of society and the Church and encourages especially young people throughout the world to treat creation and the earth's resources responsibly. *July 21*: Meeting with men and women who in their younger years were sexually abused by priests.

September 7. Pastoral visit to Cagliari at the conclusion of the centennial of the proclamation of "Our Lady of Bonaria" as patroness of Sardinia.

September 12–15. Apostolic visit to France. *September 12*: Meeting with President Nicholas Sarkozy in Paris. *September 14*: Mass in Lourdes with approximately 100,000 attending for the 150-year Jubilee of the Marian apparitions. Pope Benedict calls on Catholics to renew the missionary spirit: "To give oneself fully to God is to find the path of true freedom."

October 4. State visit with Italian President Giorgio Napolitano in the Quirinal Palace.

October 5–26. Regular General Assembly of the 12th World Synod of Bishops with the theme, "The Word of God in the Life and Mission of the Church". The Pope personally participates by giving a speech on interpretation of the Bible.

October 19. Pastoral visit to the Shrine of Our Lady of the Rosary in Pompey.

November 6. Meeting with the participants in the first Catholic-Islam dialogue, the purpose of which is to reduce tensions between the two religions.

November 9. Benedict XVI publicly commemorates in Rome the 70th anniversary of the beginning of the Jewish pogrom in Germany (*"Reichskristallnacht"*) and calls for "a profound manifestation of solidarity with the Hebrew world" and for prayer for the victims. It is the duty of each individual, he says, to oppose every form of anti-Semitism and discrimination at all levels.

November 13. Meeting with Brasilian President Luiz Inácio Lula da Silva. The discussion focuses on the question of improving the living conditions of socially marginalized sectors of the population.

2009

January 21. Decree lifting the excommunications of four bishops of the Fraternity of St. Pius X, who were consecrated by Archbishop Marcel Lefebvre in 1988 without papal mandate. Among them is Richard Williamson, who in a previously recorded interview that was now broadcast, denied that the Nazis used gas chambers.

January 28. At his general audience, the Pope gives an explanation of the Williamson case, which had caused a media scandal. He expresses his "full and unquestionable solidarity" with the Jews.

February 12. Meeting with leaders of the Conference of Presidents of Major American Jewish Organizations, in which Benedict XVI condemns anti-Semitism and clearly rejects any denial of the Holocaust.

March 10. Letter to the bishops of the Catholic Church, in which the Pope discusses misunderstandings and debates in connection with the excommunication of the four bishops of the Fraternity of St. Pius X and admits to a failure in the Vatican's public relations work.

March 17–23. Apostolic visit to Cameroon and Angola. The purpose of the journey is to bring a message of hope and reconciliation to a continent that is tormented by wars, sickness, and hunger, and to demand justice for Africa from the world community. Pope Benedict's statement that the problem of AIDS cannot be solved by condoms alone meets with criticism in the world press.

April 28. Visit to the Abruzzi region, which had been hit by an earthquake.

May 8–15. Apostolic visit to the Holy Land. *May 8:* Meeting with Jordanian King Abdullah in the Al-Husseinye Palace of Amman. *May 9:* Visit to the Byzantine Basilica of the Memorial of Moses on Mount Nebo; meeting with Muslim religious leaders. *May 10:* Visit to the site of Jesus' baptism in the Jordan. *May 11:* Visit to the Holocaust Memorial Yad Vashem in Jerusalem, together with the Israeli President Shimon Peres. In his speech, Pope Benedict declares, in reference to the murder of six million Jews in the Nazi period, "May the names of these victims never perish! May their suffering never be denied, belittled or forgotten!" *May 12:* Benedict XVI becomes the first Pope in history to visit the Muslim Dome of the Rock on the Temple Mount; meeting with the Grand Mufti of Jerusalem, Muhammad Ahmad Hussein; prayer at the Wailing Wall. *May 13:* Meeting with Palestinian President Mahmoud Abbas in Bethlehem. *May 14:*

Meeting with Prime Minister Benjamin Netanjahu in Nazareth. Mass and visit to the Grotto of the Annunciation in Nazareth. *May 15*: Visit to the Church of the Holy Sepulcher in Jerusalem.

May 24. Pastoral visit to Cassino and Montecassino, the principal abbey founded by his patron and the patron of Europe, Saint Benedict.

June 19. Beginning of the "Year for Priests" proclaimed by Benedict XVI.

June 21. Pastoral visit to San Giovanni Rotondo, place of pilgrimage and shrine of the Capuchin friar Padre Pio, who died in 1968 and was canonized in 2002.

June 29. Third encyclical, the social encyclical *Caritas in veritate* (Charity in Truth) on the consequences of globalization and of the economic and financial crisis and on an economic order that is more just, socially beneficial, and ecologically sound.

July 2. Apostolic letter in the form of a motu proprio *Ecclesiae unitatem*, with which the Pontifical Commission *Ecclesia Dei*, along with its competence for relations with traditionalist Catholics, such as the Priestly Fraternity of St. Pius X, is incorporated into the Congregation for the Doctrine of the Faith.

July 7. Apostolic letter in the form of a motu proprio approving the new Statute of the Labor Office of the Holy See.

July 9. Meeting with Australian Prime Minister Kevin Rudd. Meeting with South Korean President Lee Myung-bak to discuss the consequences of the world economic crisis for the poorest nations and the political and social situation on the Korean peninsula.

July 10. Meeting with U.S. President Barack Obama. The private audience focuses on the world economic crisis, the situation in the Near East, developmental policy in Africa and South America, as well as international efforts to combat drug trafficking. Also discussed were stem cell research, bioethics, and the problem of abortion.

July 17. Minor surgical procedure to his right hand after the Pope broke his wrist in a fall during his summer vacation in the Aosta Valley.

September 6. Pastoral visit to Viterbo and Bagnoregio. In Viterbo, the longest conclave in Church history took place (1,005 days); in Bagnoregio, the only relic of Saint Bonaventure is preserved.

September 26–28. Apostolic visit to the Czech Republic. The purpose of the visit, 20 years after the fall of the Iron Curtain, is to encourage the minority of believers and to remind them of the Christian roots of the culture of this now largely atheistic country.

October 4–25. Second Special Assembly of the Synod of Bishops for Africa.

October 26. Apostolic letter in the form of a motu proprio *Omnium in mentem*, modifying several norms of the Code of Canon Law.

November 4. Apostolic constitution *Anglicanorum coetibus* on the erection of personal ordinariates for Anglicans who enter into full communion with the Catholic Church.

November 8. Pastoral visit to Concesio and Brescia, the home of Pope Paul VI.

November 14. Meeting with the Czech Premier Jan Fischer concerning the European Union Treaty of Lisbon.

November 21. Meeting with the Archbishop of Canterbury, Rowan Williams, the Primate of the Anglican Church. The discussion centered on the challenges to the Christian community at the beginning of the third millennium.

December 3. Meeting with Russian head of State Dmitri Medvedev; announcement of the establishing of diplomatic relations between the Vatican and the Kremlin.

2010

January 1. Call for an ecological turning point: "If you want to cultivate peace, protect creation."

January 15. Letter of the rector of the Catholic *Canisius-Kolleg*, Fr. Klaus Mertes, to 600 graduates of the Jesuit preparatory school in Berlin, in which he asks for forgiveness from the victims of abuse by Jesuits at the Berlin school during the 1970s and 1980s. The publication of this letter leads to the disclosure of other cases in other Catholic and non-Catholic institutions.

January 17. Visit of the Pope to the synagogue in Rome.

February 15–16. Meeting with 24 Irish bishops to address the abuse scandal in the Catholic Church of Ireland. The Pope censures serious mistakes on the part of the bishops.

March 12. Meeting with Robert Zollitsch, Chairman of the German Bishops' Conference, in response to the great number of abuse cases in Germany.

March 14. Visit to the German-speaking Evangelical Lutheran congregation in Rome, sermon at their worship service.

March 19. Pastoral Letter to the Catholics in Ireland, in which Benedict XVI asks forgiveness for the cases of abuse at Catholic institutions and for the failure of the bishops and gives guidelines for reporting cases and responding to the crisis situation beyond Ireland.

April 17–18. Apostolic visit to Malta. The occasion is the landing of the Apostle Paul on the island 1,950 years ago. During his visit, Benedict XVI meets also with Maltese victims of abuse.

May 1. After the conclusion of the Visitation of the Legionaries of Christ that he had ordered, the Pope demands a comprehensive spiritual and structural renewal of the religious congregation.

May 2. Pastoral visit to Turin on the occasion of the exhibition of the Shroud, the sacred burial cloth of Christ.

May 11–14. Apostolic visit to Portugal. The occasion is the tenth anniversary of the beatification of the shepherd children of Fatima, Jacinta and Francisco. *May 13:* Holy Mass at the Shrine of Fatima. "I have come to Fatima to pray, in union with Mary and so many pilgrims, for our human family, afflicted as it is by various ills and sufferings."

May 20. Concert at the Vatican in collaboration with the Russian National Orchestra and the Synodal Choir of Moscow in honor of the fifth anniversary of Benedict's pontificate. The concert is a present from the Patriarch of Moscow, Kirill I, and is considered a sign of rapprochement between the Russian Orthodox and the Catholic Church.

May 31. Delegation of five high-ranking special investigators to Ireland to deal with the abuse scandal.

June 4–6. Apostolic visit to Cyprus. *June 5*: Meeting with the Orthodox Church leader Chrysostomos II. *June 6*: Delivery of the *Instrumentum Laboris* for the upcoming Special Assembly of the Synod of Bishops for the Near East.

June 10–11. Participates in what is presumably the largest meeting of priests in history at the conclusion of the Year for Priests.

June 26. Meeting with the outgoing General Secretary of the Lutheran World Federation, Ishmael Noko.

June 29. Announcement of the institution of the "Pontifical Council for Promoting the New Evangelization" for post-Christian societies.

July 4. Pastoral visit to Sulmona in the Abruzzi region on the occasion of the 800th birthday of Pope Celestine V, who after a half a year as Pope resigned from office.

September 2. Meeting with Israeli President Shimon Peres, to discuss the peace process in the Middle East. Under Benedict XVI, according to Peres, relations between the

Vatican and Israel are "the best since the time of Jesus Christ".

September 5. Visit to Carpetino Romano, the birthplace 200 years ago of Pope Leo XIII, who developed the Church's social teaching in response to the Industrial Revolution.

September 16–19. Apostolic visit to England and Scotland: the first State visit of a Pope to Great Britain. *September 16*: Meeting with Queen Elizabeth II, the head of the Anglican Church, in Edinburgh. *September 17*: Ecumenical celebration in Westminster Abbey, London. *September 19*: The beatification of the convert and cardinal John Henry Newman in Birmingham is the first beatification Mass ever on English soil.

October 3. Meeting with families and youth in Palermo, Sicily.

October 10–24. Special Assembly of the Synod of Bishops on the Situation of Christians in the Near East.

November 6–7. Pastoral visit to Spain. *November 6*: Visit to Santiago de Compostela on the occasion of the Year of St. James. *November 7*: Consecration of the altar in Holy Family Church (*La Sagrada Familia*) in Barcelona.